Super Easy
ZERO POINT
Weight Loss

COOKBOOK 2025

Diayunati Brayutuer

Lose Weight, Healthy & Delicious No
Point Recipes Book for Beginners without
Counting Calories | Incl. a 30-Day Meal
Plan for Success

TABLE OF CONTENTS

INTRODUCTION

The Super Easy Zero Point Weight Loss Cookbook 2025 is more than just a collection of recipes; it is a comprehensive resource designed to make your journey toward a healthier and more balanced lifestyle both enjoyable and sustainable. Whether you're a beginner looking to lose weight or a seasoned cook seeking fresh ideas for nutritious meals, this cookbook has something for everyone. Packed with zero-point recipes, it eliminates the need to count calories, ensuring you can focus on enjoying delicious meals while effortlessly working toward your weight loss goals.

Healthy Eating Made Simple

Healthy eating often feels complicated, with endless calorie counting, portion control, and tracking of macronutrients. This cookbook simplifies the process by offering recipes that are naturally low in calories, fat, and sodium while being rich in fiber, protein, and essential nutrients. By focusing on zero-point ingredients, it helps you create meals that are satisfying and supportive of your health goals without the stress of meticulous tracking.

Each recipe is designed to nourish your body and mind, promoting a balanced approach to eating. Forget about crash diets or restrictive eating plans—this cookbook emphasizes real, wholesome ingredients that make every bite a step toward better health.

A World of Flavorful Variety

One of the most challenging aspects of weight loss is staying motivated and avoiding food fatigue. The Super Easy Zero Point Weight Loss Cookbook 2025 addresses this by offering a wide variety of recipes inspired by global cuisines. From exotic dishes like Ethiopian chicken with cauliflower to Asian-style vegetable stir-fries, and classic American comfort foods reimagined in a healthy way, this cookbook ensures your meals are never boring.

Each recipe is thoughtfully crafted to balance flavor, texture, and nutrition. Imagine starting your day with a refreshing fruit and yogurt parfait, enjoying a light yet satisfying lunch of roasted vegetable salad, and ending your evening with a hearty, zero-point soup. With so many options, you'll always have something new and exciting to try.

Convenience for Busy Lifestyles

In today's fast-paced world, time is a precious commodity. Preparing healthy meals can feel like an overwhelming task, but this cookbook is here to prove otherwise. Each recipe is designed with convenience in mind, featuring minimal prep time, straightforward instructions, and ingredients that are easy to find at your local grocery store. Whether you're a working professional, a busy parent, or someone who simply values their time, this cookbook ensures that healthy eating fits seamlessly into your schedule.

Additionally, the book provides detailed information for each recipe, including preparation and cooking times, serving sizes, and nutritional details. You'll know exactly what you're eating and how long it will take to make, giving you the confidence to plan your meals efficiently.

Empowering a Healthier Lifestyle

The Super Easy Zero Point Weight Loss Cookbook 2025 isn't just about weight loss; it's about creating a sustainable and enjoyable lifestyle. By focusing on nutrient-rich, whole foods, the recipes support overall wellness, from boosting your energy levels to improving your mood. Eating well becomes a natural part of your day rather than a chore, helping you maintain your progress in the long term.

The cookbook also emphasizes mindful eating practices. By slowing down and savoring your meals, you'll not only enjoy the flavors but also tune into your body's hunger and fullness cues. This approach fosters a healthier relationship with food and encourages you to view it as a source of nourishment and pleasure rather than a cause for stress.

Perfect for Beginners and Seasoned Cooks Alike

Whether you're new to cooking or a culinary enthusiast, the Super Easy Zero Point Weight Loss Cookbook 2025 caters to all skill levels. Beginners will appreciate the clear instructions and accessible ingredients, while experienced cooks will enjoy experimenting with the diverse flavors and creative combinations. The recipes are designed to be flexible, allowing you to adjust seasonings, swap ingredients, or scale up portions to suit your preferences.

The cookbook is also a great resource for families or anyone cooking for multiple people. Many recipes include options for scaling up to serve larger groups, ensuring that everyone at the table can enjoy healthy, zero-point meals together.

Achieve Your Goals Without Sacrifice

The Super Easy Zero Point Weight Loss Cookbook 2025 proves that healthy eating doesn't mean giving up the foods you love. By focusing on creative, flavorful recipes, it allows you to enjoy satisfying meals while staying on track with your weight loss goals. Say goodbye to the days of boring salads and flavorless diet foods—this cookbook celebrates the joy of eating well and feeling great.

Your Path to Success Starts Here

With its user-friendly format, diverse recipes, and practical tips, the Super Easy Zero Point Weight Loss Cookbook 2025 is your ultimate guide to a healthier, happier lifestyle. By simplifying the process of meal planning and preparation, it ensures that healthy eating becomes an enjoyable part of your routine. Whether you're aiming to lose weight, maintain your progress, or simply explore new ways to cook nutritious meals, this cookbook is here to support you every step of the way.

Transform your kitchen, your health, and your life—one delicious, zero-point recipe at a time.

Chapter 1

Embracing Sustainable Weight Loss

easier and more enjoyable.

What sets this approach apart is its flexibility. Rather than restricting entire food groups or relying on processed substitutes, zero-point recipes celebrate whole, natural ingredients. This creates a foundation for sustainable eating habits that align with your weight loss goals.

The Nutritional Foundation of Zero-Point Recipes

Zero-point recipes are built on foods that are nutrient-dense, meaning they provide essential vitamins and minerals without adding excessive calories. This balance is key to their effectiveness. For example:

1. High Fiber Content: Many zero-point foods, such as vegetables and legumes, are rich in dietary fiber. Fiber supports digestion, regulates blood sugar levels, and promotes a feeling of fullness, helping you avoid overeating.

2. Lean Proteins: Proteins like chicken breast, fish, and tofu form the backbone of many zero-point meals. They support muscle growth and repair while keeping you satisfied for longer periods.

3. Low Glycemic Index: Zero-point recipes often incorporate foods with a low glycemic index, which helps stabilize blood sugar levels and reduces cravings.

By combining these elements, zero-point recipes nourish your body while supporting your weight loss journey. They're not just about eating less—they're about eating smarter.

Why Zero-Point Recipes Work for Weight Loss

One of the greatest challenges in weight loss is maintaining a calorie deficit while avoiding hunger and cravings. Zero-point recipes address this by prioritizing foods that naturally promote satiety. By eating meals that are rich in fiber, protein, and water content, you can enjoy larger portions without exceeding your calorie goals.

For example, consider a meal centered around roasted vegetables and grilled chicken. This combination delivers plenty of volume and flavor while being low in calories. The high water and fiber content of the vegetables paired with the protein in the chicken ensures you stay full and satisfied, reducing the temptation to snack on less nutritious options.

Additionally, zero-point recipes work with your body rather than against it. Instead of triggering restrictive eating behaviors that can lead to burnout, they encourage a balanced approach to nutrition. This makes it easier to stay consistent over time, which is the key to long-term success.

The Super Easy Zero Point Weight Loss Cookbook 2025 is built on the concept of zero-point recipes, a revolutionary approach to eating that simplifies weight loss without sacrificing flavor or satisfaction. In this chapter, we'll explore the principles that make zero-point recipes effective, the nutritional benefits they offer, and how incorporating them into your lifestyle can lead to long-term success.

The Concept of Zero Points

At its core, the zero-point philosophy is about focusing on foods that are naturally low in calories but high in nutritional value. Unlike traditional calorie counting, which can be tedious and discouraging, zero-point recipes simplify the process by emphasizing foods that you can enjoy without guilt or strict portion control.

Zero-point recipes are designed around ingredients that your body processes efficiently, keeping you full and energized while promoting healthy weight loss. These meals eliminate the need for weighing or measuring certain foods, making meal preparation

How to Integrate Zero-Point Recipes into Your Routine

Incorporating zero-point recipes into your daily life doesn't require an overhaul of your current habits. Instead, it's about making small, sustainable changes that fit seamlessly into your routine. Here are a few strategies to get started:

1. Plan Ahead: Take time to plan your meals for the week. Choose a mix of zero-point breakfast, lunch, and dinner recipes to keep things interesting. Meal prepping can save time and ensure you always have healthy options on hand.

2. Focus on Balance: While zero-point foods are a great foundation, it's important to pair them with healthy fats and whole grains to create balanced meals. This approach ensures you're getting all the nutrients your body needs.

3. Experiment with Flavors: Use herbs, spices, and citrus to add depth and complexity to your meals. Zero-point recipes are anything but boring, and experimenting with flavors can make cooking more enjoyable.

By adopting these habits, you'll find that zero-point recipes become a natural part of your lifestyle, making it easier to achieve and maintain your health goals.

The Long-Term Benefits of Zero-Point Recipes

Beyond weight loss, zero-point recipes offer a host of long-term benefits that contribute to overall well-being. These include:

1. Improved Energy Levels: By focusing on nutrient-dense ingredients, zero-point meals provide sustained energy throughout the day, helping you stay productive and active.

2. Better Digestion: The high fiber content in many zero-point foods supports a healthy digestive system, reducing bloating and promoting regularity.

3. Enhanced Mood: Eating well-balanced meals can have a positive impact on your mental health, reducing stress and improving your overall outlook.

Perhaps most importantly, zero-point recipes foster a positive relationship with food. Instead of viewing meals as a source of stress or guilt, you'll begin to see them as an opportunity to nourish your body and enjoy the process of eating.

A New Way of Eating

The zero-point philosophy is more than a tool for weight loss—it's a mindset shift that transforms the way you think about food. By focusing on ingredients that support your health and satisfaction, zero-point recipes make it possible to achieve your goals without sacrificing flavor or enjoyment.

As you explore the recipes in this cookbook, remember that every meal is an opportunity to care for your body and mind. Whether you're preparing a quick weeknight dinner or experimenting with a new dish, you'll discover that eating well doesn't have to be complicated or restrictive. With zero-point recipes, healthy eating becomes an accessible, sustainable part of your daily life—one delicious bite at a time.

30-Day Meal Plan

DAYS	BREAKFAST	LUNCH	DINNER	SNACK/DESSERT
1	Cauliflower and Nut Porridge	Braised Chicken with Olives	Spiced Beef Shami Kabob	Pecan Clusters
2	Spicy Cajun Breakfast Sausage	Juicy Pork Meatballs	Fiery Spiced Lamb Sirloin Chops	Instant Protein Ice Cream
3	Cheesy Cheddar Chicken Casserole	Spicy Chili Lamb Soup	Beef Tripe Stir-Fried with Vegetables	Toasted Coconut Marshmallows
4	Greek Yogurt Delight	Creamy Shrimp Chowder	Chilean Sea Bass with Olive Relish	Raspberry Cheesecake
5	Bite-Sized Chocolate Chip Muffins	Ethiopian Chicken with Cauliflower	Easygoing Meatloaf	Bacon Fudge
6	Savory Mushroom Frittata	Spicy Avocado and Serrano Chile Soup	Hearty Beef and Red Cabbage Stew	Coconut Flour Cake
7	Hearty Bacon, Spinach, and Avocado Egg Wrap	Classic New England Clam Chowder	Garam Masala Fish	Candied Mixed Nuts
8	Flapjack Treats	Turkey Meatloaf Florentine Muffins	Fish and Scallop Ceviche	No-Bake N'Oatmeal Chocolate Chip Cookies
9	Quick Skillet Pancakes	Chili Lime Turkey Burgers	Lemon Butter Mahi Mahi	Peanut Butter Hemp Heart Cookies
10	Spinach and Egg Omelet	Thai Tacos with Peanut Sauce	Almond Catfish	Egg Custard Tarts
11	Berry Bliss Smoothie	Hearty Green Minestrone Soup	Beef Steak Topped with Cheesy Mushroom Sauce	Chocolate Cake with Walnuts
12	Rustic Cowboy Breakfast Skillet	Chipotle Drumsticks	Rainbow Salmon Kebabs	Crustless Cheesecake Bites
13	Unique Boiled Eggs	Cheddar and Sausage Beer Soup	Louisiana Shrimp Gumbo	Coconut Lemon Squares
14	Hearty Sausage, Spinach, and Goat Cheese Bake	Savory Mushroom Pizza Soup	Pork Rind Salmon Cakes	Snickerdoodle Cream Cheesecake
15	Kale Spread	Chicken and Scallions Stuffed Peppers	Stuffed Trout	Orange–Olive Oil Cupcakes
16	Cheesy Egg Muffins	Rich and Creamy Mushroom Soup	Lime Lobster Tails	Coconut Muffins

DAYS	BREAKFAST	LUNCH	DINNER	SNACK/DESSERT
17	Pizza-Style Eggs	Spice-Rubbed Chicken Thighs	Oregano Tilapia Fingers	Peanut Butter Cookies
18	Crispy Bacon Crackers	Fresh Summer Vegetable Soup	Classic Fish Sticks with Tartar Sauce	Vanilla Cream Pie
19	Pork and Quill Egg Bites	Savory Beef Meatball Stroganoff	Spicy Grilled Shrimp with Mojo Verde	Double Chocolate Brownies
20	Overnight Oatless Delight	Herb-Infused Rosemary Pork Belly	Tuna Salad with Tomatoes and Peppers	Almond Chai Truffles
21	Veggie and Beef Hash with Eggs	Roasted Garlic Beef	Greek Shrimp with Tomatoes and Feta	Pecan Brownies
22	Avocado Eggs	Cuban-Style Pork Shoulder	Baked Monkfish	Crustless Peanut Butter Cheesecake
23	Spiced Pumpkin Muffins	Hearty Ground Beef Cabbage Bake	Trout and Fennel Parcels	Baked Cheesecake
24	All-Inclusive Bagels	Flavorful Pork Wraps	Tuna Patties with Spicy Sriracha Sauce	Crustless Creamy Berry Cheesecake
25	Cheddar Sausage and Egg Muffins	Crispy Golden Bacon Strips	Baked Tilapia and Parmesan	Keto Brownies
26	Almond Meal Pancakes	Pork Tenderloin with Creamy Avocado Lime Sauce	Curried Fish Stew	Berry Cheesecake Fat Bomb
27	Salmon and Bacon Rolls with Sauce	Zesty Mustard Lamb Chops	Chunky Fish Soup with Tomatoes	Fruit Pizza
28	Creamy Cheese Muffins	Savory Beef Sausage Meat Loaf	Chili Tilapia	Coconut Chocolate Cookies
29	Creamy Mushroom and Cheese Lettuce Wraps	Fajita-Style Pork Shoulder	Coconut Curry Mussels	Strawberry Shortcake Coconut Sorbet
30	Low-Carb English Muffins	Parmesan-Crusted Chicken	White Fish with Cauliflower	Delightful Jelly Cups

Chapter 2

Breakfasts

Cauliflower and Nut Porridge

- ◆ 2½ cups water, divided
- ◆ ½ cup raw cashews
- ◆ ½ cup almond slivers
- ◆ ¼ cup raw pumpkin seeds

Topping:

- ◆ ¼ cup hemp seeds
- ◆ ¼ cup chia seeds
- ◆ ¼ head cauliflower, chopped
- ◆ Sea salt, to taste
- ◆ ¼ cup heavy whipping cream
- ◆ 1 tablespoon cinnamon

1. In a small bowl, add 2 cups of the water, the cashews, almonds and pumpkin seeds. Soak for 30 minutes. Drain the water and set aside. Reserve a few nuts and pumpkin seeds in a separate bowl to be used as garnish. 2. Pour the remaining ½ cup of the water into the Instant Pot and add the soaked nuts mixture, cauliflower and sea salt. 3. Lock the lid. Select the Manual mode and set the cooking time for 5 minutes at High Pressure. When the timer goes off, use a natural pressure release for 10 minutes, then release any remaining pressure. Carefully open the lid. 4. Transfer the cauliflower and nuts mixture to a food processor, add the heavy cream and pulse until smooth. 5. Season with a pinch of sea salt. Garnish with the reserved nuts, pumpkin seeds, hemp seeds and chia seeds and sprinkle with the cinnamon. Serve immediately.

Per Serving:

calories: 368 | fat: 30g | protein: 15g | carbs: 16g | net carbs: 8g | fiber: 8g

Spicy Cajun Breakfast Sausage

- ◆ 1½ pounds (680 g) 85% lean ground turkey
- ◆ 3 cloves garlic, finely chopped
- ◆ ¼ onion, grated
- ◆ 1 teaspoon Tabasco sauce
- ◆ 1 teaspoon Creole seasoning
- ◆ 1 teaspoon dried thyme
- ◆ ½ teaspoon paprika
- ◆ ½ teaspoon cayenne

1. Preheat the air fryer to 370°F (188°C). 2. In a large bowl, combine the turkey, garlic, onion, Tabasco, Creole seasoning, thyme, paprika, and cayenne. Mix with clean hands until thoroughly combined. Shape into 16 patties, about ½ inch thick. (Wet your hands slightly if you find the sausage too sticky to handle.) 3. Working in batches if necessary, arrange the patties in a single layer in the air fryer basket. Pausing halfway through the cooking time to flip the patties, air fry for 15 to 20 minutes until a thermometer

inserted into the thickest portion registers 165°F (74°C).

Per Serving:

calories: 164 | fat: 9g | protein: 19g | carbs: 2g | net carbs: 2g | fiber: 0g

Cheesy Cheddar Chicken Casserole

- ◆ 1 cup ground chicken
- ◆ 1 teaspoon olive oil
- ◆ 1 teaspoon chili flakes
- ◆ 1 teaspoon salt
- ◆ 1 cup shredded Cheddar cheese
- ◆ ½ cup coconut cream

1. Press the Sauté button on the Instant Pot and heat the oil. Add the ground chicken, chili flakes and salt to the pot and sauté for 10 minutes. Stir in the remaining ingredients. 2. Set the lid in place. Select the Manual mode and set the cooking time for 10 minutes on High Pressure. When the timer goes off, do a quick pressure release. Carefully open the lid. 3. Let the dish cool for 10 minutes before serving.

Per Serving:

calories: 172 | fat: 13g | protein: 12g | carbs: 1g | net carbs: 1g | fiber: 1g

Greek Yogurt Delight

- ◆ ½ cup plain whole-milk Greek yogurt
- ◆ 2 tablespoons heavy whipping cream
- ◆ ¼ cup frozen berries, thawed with juices
- ◆ ½ teaspoon vanilla or
- almond extract (optional)
- ◆ ¼ teaspoon ground cinnamon (optional)
- ◆ 1 tablespoon ground flaxseed
- ◆ 2 tablespoons chopped nuts (walnuts or pecans)

1. In a small bowl or glass, combine the yogurt, heavy whipping cream, thawed berries in their juice, vanilla or almond extract (if using), cinnamon (if using), and flaxseed and stir well until smooth. Top with chopped nuts and enjoy.

Per Serving:

calories: 401 | fat: 32g | protein: 15g | carbs: 16g | net carbs: 11g | fiber: 5g

Berry Bliss Smoothie

Prep time: 5 minutes | Cook time: 0 minutes | Serves 5

- 2 cups unsweetened vanilla almond milk
- 2 cups (9 ounces / 255 g) raspberries, fresh or frozen
- 1 cup (3½ ounces / 99 g) blueberries, fresh or frozen
- ½ cup monk fruit/erythritol

- sweetener blend (1:1 sugar replacement)
- ½ cup almond butter, no sugar added
- ½ cup lemon juice
- ¼ cup chia seeds

1. In a blender, combine all the ingredients and blend until smooth. If using fresh berries, chill the smoothie for 30 minutes.

Per Serving:
calories: 256 | fat: 18g | protein: 8g | carbs: 39g | net carbs: 11g | fiber: 28g

Rustic Cowboy Breakfast Skillet

Prep time: 20 minutes | Cook time: 42 minutes | serves 8

Crust:

- 1 (12-ounce) bag frozen riced cauliflower
- 1 large egg

Filling:

- 8 ounces bulk breakfast sausage
- 6 slices bacon, chopped
- ½ cup diced bell peppers (any color)
- 2 tablespoons chopped

- ½ cup grated Parmesan cheese
- ¼ teaspoon salt

- green onions
- 6 large eggs
- ¼ teaspoon salt
- ½ teaspoon ground black pepper

To make the crust: 1. Preheat the oven to 425°F. Grease a 12-inch cast-iron skillet or other ovenproof skillet with oil. 2. Cook the cauliflower according to the package directions. Allow to cool slightly, then use cheesecloth or paper towels to absorb any excess water. 3. In a medium-sized bowl, mix together the cooked cauliflower, egg, Parmesan cheese, and salt. Press the mixture evenly across the bottom of the prepared skillet. Par-bake the crust for 12 minutes or until it starts to brown around the edges, then remove from the oven and set aside to cool. Leave the oven on. While the crust is baking, make the filling. To make the filling: 1. In a skillet over medium heat, cook the sausage, bacon, bell peppers, and green onions, crumbling the sausage with a large spoon as it cooks, until the meats are fully cooked and the vegetables are tender, about 10 minutes. Remove from the heat and set aside. 2. In a medium-sized bowl, whisk together the eggs, salt, and pepper.

Add the meat mixture to the eggs and stir until well combined. 3. Pour the filling over the cooled, par-baked crust and spread evenly. 4. Return the skillet to the oven and bake for 20 minutes or until the eggs are set and slightly firm to the touch. Run a knife around the edge of the skillet before slicing. Serve immediately. Leftovers can be stored in the refrigerator for up to 5 days. Reheat just until warmed; be careful not to overheat or the eggs will become rubbery.

Per Serving:
calories: 338 | fat: 26g | protein: 20g | carbs: 6g | net carbs: 3g | fiber: 3g

Avocado Eggs

Prep time: 5 minutes | Cook time: 35 minutes | Serves 2

- 1 large avocado, halved and pitted
- 2 small eggs
- Pink Himalayan sea salt

- Freshly ground black pepper
- 1 bacon slice, cooked until crispy and crumbled

1. Preheat the oven to 375ºF (190ºC). 2. Using a small spoon, enlarge the hole of the avocado left by the pit so it is roughly 2 inches in diameter. 3. Place the avocado halves cut-side up on a baking sheet. 4. Crack an egg into the well of each half. Season with salt and pepper. 5. Bake for 30 to 35 minutes, until the yolk reaches your preferred texture, 30 minutes for soft and 35 minutes for hard. 6. Sprinkle the bacon crumbles on top and enjoy!

Per Serving:
calories: 264 | fat: 21g | protein: 10g | carbs: 12g | net carbs: 3g | fiber: 9g

Overnight Oatless Delight

Prep time: 5 minutes | Cook time: 0 minutes | Serves 1

- 2 tablespoons hulled hemp seeds
- 1 tablespoon chia seeds

- ½ scoop collagen powder
- ½ cup unsweetened nut or seed milk (hemp, almond, coconut, cashew)

1. In a small mason jar or glass container, combine the hemp seeds, chia seeds, collagen, and milk. 2. Secure tightly with a lid, shake well, and refrigerate overnight.

Per Serving:
calories: 263 | fat: 19g | protein: 16g | carbs: 7g | net carbs: 2g | fiber: 5g

Cheddar Sausage and Egg Muffins

Prep time: 10 minutes | Cook time: 30 minutes | Makes 12 muffins

- Nonstick cooking spray (optional)
- 8 large eggs
- 6 ounces (170 g) cream cheese
- 2 tablespoons butter
- ½ teaspoon freshly ground black pepper
- ½ teaspoon garlic powder
- 4 ounces (113 g) cooked breakfast sausage
- ½ cup grated Cheddar cheese

1. Preheat the oven to 350°F (180°C). Prepare a 12-cup muffin pan with cooking spray or cupcake liners and set aside. 2. In a blender or with a hand mixer, mix the eggs, cream cheese, butter, pepper, and garlic powder until fluffy. 3. Divide the mixture evenly between the prepared muffin cups. 4. Sprinkle each cup evenly with the sausage and cheese. 5. Bake for 30 minutes. Serve warm.

Per Serving:

1 muffin: calories: 168 | fat: 15g | protein: 7g | carbs: 1g | net carbs: 1g | fiber: 0g

Creamy Cheese Muffins

Prep time: 10 minutes | Cook time: 10 minutes | Makes 6 muffins

- 4 tablespoons melted butter, plus more for the muffin tin
- 1 cup almond flour
- ¾ tablespoon baking powder
- 2 large eggs, lightly beaten
- 2 ounces cream cheese mixed with 2 tablespoons heavy (whipping) cream
- Handful shredded Mexican blend cheese

1. Preheat the oven to 400°F. Coat six cups of a muffin tin with butter. 2. In a small bowl, mix together the almond flour and baking powder. 3. In a medium bowl, mix together the eggs, cream cheese–heavy cream mixture, shredded cheese, and 4 tablespoons of the melted butter. 4. Pour the flour mixture into the egg mixture, and beat with a hand mixer until thoroughly mixed. 5. Pour the batter into the prepared muffin cups. 6. Bake for 12 minutes, or until golden brown on top, and serve.

Per Serving:

calories: 247 | fat: 23g | protein: 8g | carbs: 4g | net carbs: 4g | fiber: 2g

Salmon and Bacon Rolls with Sauce

Prep time: 10 minutes | Cook time: 10 minutes | Makes 16 rolls

- 8 strips bacon (about 8 ounces/225 g)

Dipping Sauce:

- ½ cup (105 g) mayonnaise
- 8 ounces (225 g) smoked salmon, cut into 16 squares
- 2 tablespoons sugar-free barbecue sauce

Special Equipmnt:

- Toothpicks

1. Cook the bacon in a large frying pan over medium heat until much of the fat is rendered and the bacon is lightly browned but not crispy, 8 to 10 minutes. (You want the bacon to remain pliable so that you can bend it.) 2. Cut the cooked bacon in half lengthwise to create 16 narrow strips. Place a square of salmon on one end of a bacon strip. Roll the salmon in the bacon, secure with a toothpick, and place on a clean plate. Repeat with the remaining bacon and salmon, making a total of 16 rolls. 3. Make the dipping sauce: Place the mayonnaise and barbecue sauce in a small bowl and stir to combine. Serve alongside the salmon rolls.

Per Serving:

calories: 324 | fat: 29g | protein: 14g | carbs: 3g | net carbs: 2g | fiber: 1g

Flapjack Treats

Prep time: 10 minutes | Cook time: 14 minutes | Serves 6

- 1 cup blanched almond flour
- ¼ cup coconut flour
- 5 large eggs, whisked
- 3 (1-gram) packets 0g net carb sweetener
- 1 teaspoon baking powder
- ⅓ cup unsweetened almond milk
- ¼ cup vegetable oil
- 1½ teaspoons pure vanilla extract
- ⅛ teaspoon salt

1. In a large mixing bowl, mix all ingredients together until smooth. 2. In a large nonstick skillet over medium heat, pour desired-sized pancakes and cook 3 to 5 minutes until bubbles form. 3. Flip pancakes and cook another 2 minutes until brown. Repeat as needed to use all batter. Serve.

Per Serving:

calories: 273 | fat: 23g | protein: 10g | carbs: 7g | net carbs: 3g | fiber: 4g

Spiced Pumpkin Muffins

Prep time: 10 minutes | Cook time: 15 minutes | Serves 6

- 1 cup blanched finely ground almond flour
- ½ cup granular erythritol
- ½ teaspoon baking powder
- ¼ cup unsalted butter, softened
- ¼ cup pure pumpkin purée
- ½ teaspoon ground cinnamon
- ¼ teaspoon ground nutmeg
- 1 teaspoon vanilla extract
- 2 large eggs

1. In a large bowl, mix almond flour, erythritol, baking powder, butter, pumpkin purée, cinnamon, nutmeg, and vanilla. 2. Gently stir in eggs. 3. Evenly pour the batter into six silicone muffin cups. Place muffin cups into the air fryer basket, working in batches if necessary. 4. Adjust the temperature to 300ºF (149ºC) and bake for 15 minutes. 5. When completely cooked, a toothpick inserted in center will come out mostly clean. Serve warm.

Per Serving:
calories: 207 | fat: 18g | protein: 6g | carbs: 6g | net carbs: 2g | fiber: 4g

Quick Skillet Pancakes

Prep time: 5 minutes | Cook time: 5 minutes | Makes 8 pancakes

- 8 ounces (227 g) cream cheese
- 8 eggs
- 2 tablespoons coconut flour
- 2 teaspoons baking powder
- 1 teaspoon ground
- cinnamon
- ½ teaspoon vanilla extract
- 1 teaspoon liquid stevia or sweetener of choice (optional)
- 2 tablespoons butter

1. In a blender, combine the cream cheese, eggs, coconut flour, baking powder, cinnamon, vanilla, and stevia (if using). Blend until smooth. 2. In a large skillet over medium heat, melt the butter. 3. Use half the mixture to pour four evenly sized pancakes and cook for about a minute, until you see bubbles on top. Flip the pancakes and cook for another minute. Remove from the pan and add more butter or oil to the skillet if needed. Repeat with the remaining batter. 4. Top with butter and eat right away, or freeze the pancakes in a freezer-safe resealable bag with sheets of parchment in between, for up to 1 month.

Per Serving:
1 pancake: calories: 179 | fat: 15g | protein: 8g | carbs: 3g | net carbs: 2g | fiber: 1g

Spinach and Egg Omelet

Prep time: 5 minutes | Cook time: 12 minutes | Serves 2

- 4 large eggs
- 1½ cups chopped fresh spinach leaves
- 2 tablespoons peeled and chopped yellow onion
- 2 tablespoons salted butter, melted
- ½ cup shredded mild Cheddar cheese
- ¼ teaspoon salt

1. In an ungreased round nonstick baking dish, whisk eggs. Stir in spinach, onion, butter, Cheddar, and salt. 2. Place dish into air fryer basket. Adjust the temperature to 320ºF (160ºC) and bake for 12 minutes. Omelet will be done when browned on the top and firm in the middle. 3. Slice in half and serve warm on two medium plates.

Per Serving:
calories: 380 | fat: 31g | protein: 21g | carbs: 4g | net carbs: 3g | fiber: 1g

Hearty Bacon, Spinach, and Avocado Egg Wrap

Prep time: 10 minutes | Cook time: 10 minutes | Serves 2

- 6 bacon slices
- 2 large eggs
- 2 tablespoons heavy (whipping) cream
- Pink Himalayan salt
- Freshly ground black pepper
- 1 tablespoon butter, if needed
- 1 cup fresh spinach (or other greens of your choice)
- ½ avocado, sliced

1. In a medium skillet over medium-high heat, cook the bacon on both sides until crispy, about 8 minutes. Transfer the bacon to a paper towel–lined plate. 2. In a medium bowl, whisk the eggs and cream, and season with pink Himalayan salt and pepper. Whisk again to combine. 3. Add half the egg mixture to the skillet with the bacon grease. 4. Cook the egg mixture for about 1 minute, or until set, then flip with a spatula and cook the other side for 1 minute. 5. Transfer the cooked-egg mixture to a paper towel–lined plate to soak up extra grease. 6. Repeat steps 4 and 5 for the other half of the egg mixture. If the pan gets dry, add the butter. 7. Place a cooked egg mixture on each of two warmed plates. Top each with half of the spinach, bacon, and avocado slices. 8. Season with pink Himalayan salt and pepper, and roll the wraps. Serve hot.

Per Serving:
calories: 336 | fat: 29g | protein: 17g | carbs: 5g | net carbs: 2g | fiber: 3g

Savory Mushroom Frittata

- 2 tablespoons olive oil
- 1 cup sliced fresh mushrooms
- 1 cup shredded spinach
- 6 bacon slices, cooked and
- chopped
- 10 large eggs, beaten
- ½ cup crumbled goat cheese
- Sea salt
- Freshly ground black pepper

1. Preheat the oven to 350°F. 2. Place a large ovenproof skillet over medium-high heat and add the olive oil. 3. Sauté the mushrooms until lightly browned, about 3 minutes. 4. Add the spinach and bacon and sauté until the greens are wilted, about 1 minute. 5. Add the eggs and cook, lifting the edges of the frittata with a spatula so uncooked egg flows underneath, for 3 to 4 minutes. 6. Sprinkle the top with the crumbled goat cheese and season lightly with salt and pepper. 7. Bake until set and lightly browned, about 15 minutes. 8. Remove the frittata from the oven, and let it stand for 5 minutes. 9. Cut into 6 wedges and serve immediately.

Per Serving:

calories: 379 | fat: 27g | protein: 16g | carbs: 1g | net carbs: 1g | fiber: 0g

Almond Meal Pancakes

- 2 cups (8 ounces / 227 g) blanched almond flour
- ¼ cup erythritol
- 1 tablespoon baking powder
- ¼ teaspoon sea salt
- 4 large eggs
- ⅔ cup unsweetened almond milk
- ¼ cup avocado oil, plus more for frying
- 2 teaspoons vanilla extract

1. In a blender, combine all ingredients and blend until smooth. Let the batter rest for 5 to 10 minutes. 2. Preheat a large, very lightly oiled skillet over medium-low heat. (Keep oil very minimal for perfectly round pancakes.) Working in batches, pour circles of batter onto the pan, 2 tablespoons (⅛ cup) at a time for 3-inch pancakes. Cook 1½ to 2 minutes, until bubbles start to form on the edges. Flip and cook another minute or two, until browned on the other side. 3. Repeat with the remaining batter.

Per Serving:

calories: 355 | fat: 31g | protein: 12g | carbs: 12g | net carbs: 5g | fiber: 7g

Bite-Sized Chocolate Chip Muffins

- 1 cup blanched almond flour
- 2 eggs
- ¾ cup sugar-free chocolate chips
- 1 tablespoon vanilla extract
- ½ cup Swerve, or more to taste
- 2 tablespoons salted grass-fed butter, softened
- ½ teaspoon salt
- ¼ teaspoon baking soda

1. Pour 1 cup of filtered water into the inner pot of the Instant Pot, then insert the trivet. Using an electric mixer, combine flour, eggs, chocolate chips, vanilla, Swerve, butter, salt, and baking soda. Mix thoroughly. Transfer this mixture into a well-greased Instant Pot-friendly muffin (or egg bites) mold. 2. Using a sling if desired, place the pan onto the trivet and cover loosely with aluminum foil. Close the lid, set the pressure release to Sealing, and select Manual. Set the Instant Pot to 20 minutes on High Pressure and let cook. 3. Once cooked, let the pressure naturally disperse from the Instant Pot for about 10 minutes, then carefully switch the pressure release to Venting. 4. Open the Instant Pot and remove the pan. Let cool, serve, and enjoy!

Per Serving:

calories: 204 | fat: 17g | protein: 3g | carbs: 10g | net carbs: 9g | fiber: 1g

Cheesy Egg Muffins

- 4 eggs
- 2 tablespoons heavy cream
- ¼ teaspoon salt
- ⅛ teaspoon pepper
- ⅓ cup shredded Cheddar cheese
- 1 cup water

1. In a large bowl, whisk eggs and heavy cream. Add salt and pepper. 2. Pour mixture into 6 silicone cupcake baking molds. Sprinkle cheese into each cup. 3. Pour water into Instant Pot and place steam rack in bottom of pot. Carefully set filled silicone molds steadily on steam rack. If all do not fit, separate into two batches. 4. Click lid closed. Press the Manual button and adjust time for 10 minutes. When timer beeps, allow a quick release and remove lid. Egg bites will look puffy at first, but will become smaller once they begin to cool. Serve warm.

Per Serving:

calories: 90 | fat: 6g | protein: 6g | carbs: 1g | net carbs: 1g | fiber: 0g

Crispy Bacon Crackers

♦ 13 strips bacon (about 13 ounces/370 g), preferably thick-cut

1. Preheat the oven to 400°F (205°C) and line a rimmed baking sheet with parchment paper or a silicone baking mat. 2. Cut the strips of bacon into roughly 2-inch (5-cm) squares, about 6 per strip. Place the squares on the prepared baking sheet, leaving a small gap between crackers. 3. Bake the crackers until crisp, about 15 minutes if using regular bacon or 20 minutes if using thick-cut bacon. 4. Allow the crackers to cool on the baking sheet for 10 minutes. Transfer to a serving plate and enjoy.

Per Serving:

calories: 258 | fat: 25g | protein: 8g | carbs: 1g | net carbs: 1g | fiber: 0g

Unique Boiled Eggs

Boiled Eggs:

♦ 10 eggs

♦ 1 tablespoon coconut vinegar or apple cider vinegar

Sauce:

♦ 1½ cups water

♦ 2 tablespoons liquid aminos or tamari

♦ 2 tablespoons coconut aminos

♦ 2 tablespoons coconut vinegar or apple cider vinegar

♦ 1 teaspoon minced fresh garlic or garlic powder

♦ 1 teaspoon minced fresh ginger or ground ginger

♦ 1 teaspoon sea salt

♦ ½ teaspoon freshly ground black pepper

Make the Boiled Eggs: 1. Place the eggs in a medium pot and add enough cold water to cover them. Add a splash of vinegar (this makes the eggs easier to peel) and bring to a boil. When the water boils, remove the pot from the heat, cover, and let sit for 10 minutes. 2. Meanwhile, fill a large bowl with water and ice. When the eggs are done, transfer them to the ice bath for another 10 minutes. 3. Peel the eggs and set them aside. Make the Sauce: 4. In a large storage bowl with a lid, whisk together the water, liquid aminos, coconut aminos, vinegar, garlic, ginger, salt, and pepper. Alternatively, you can divide the ingredients in half and add to two large mason jars with lids. 5. Place the peeled eggs in the sauce. Cover and refrigerate. The longer the eggs soak up the sauce, the more flavorful they will be.

Per Serving:

2 eggs: calories: 144 | fat: 10g | protein: 12g | carbs: 2g | net carbs: 2g | fiber: 0g

Pizza-Style Eggs

♦ 1 cup shredded Mozzarella cheese

♦ 7 slices pepperoni, chopped

♦ 1 large egg, whisked

♦ ¼ teaspoon dried oregano

♦ ¼ teaspoon dried parsley

♦ ¼ teaspoon garlic powder

♦ ¼ teaspoon salt

1. Place Mozzarella in a single layer on the bottom of an ungreased round nonstick baking dish. Scatter pepperoni over cheese, then pour egg evenly around baking dish. 2. Sprinkle with remaining ingredients and place into air fryer basket. Adjust the temperature to 330°F (166°C) and bake for 10 minutes. When cheese is brown and egg is set, dish will be done. 3. Let cool in dish 5 minutes before serving.

Per Serving:

calories: 240 | fat: 18g | protein: 17g | carbs: 2g | net carbs: 2g | fiber: 0g

Kale Spread

♦ 2 tablespoons refined avocado oil, for the pan

♦ 4 cups (190 g) chopped kale

♦ ½ cup (75 g) sesame seeds

♦ ½ cup (120 ml) refined avocado oil or extra-virgin olive oil

♦ 8 green onions, green parts only, roughly chopped

♦ 3 tablespoons apple cider vinegar

♦ 1¼ teaspoons finely ground gray sea salt

1. Place 2 tablespoons of avocado oil and the chopped kale in a large frying pan over medium heat. Cover and cook until the kale is slightly crispy, stirring occasionally, 3 to 6 minutes. 2. Meanwhile, place the remaining ingredients in a blender or food processor.

Per Serving:

calories: 228 | fat: 22g | protein: 3g | carbs: 6g | net carbs: 4g | fiber: 2g

Veggie and Beef Hash with Eggs

Prep time: 5 minutes | Cook time: 35 minutes | Serves 4

- 2 tablespoons good-quality olive oil
- ½ pound grass-fed ground beef
- ½ red bell pepper, diced
- ½ zucchini, diced
- ¼ onion, diced
- 2 teaspoons minced garlic
- 1½ cups low-carb tomato sauce
- 1 tablespoon dried basil
- 1 teaspoon dried oregano
- ⅛ teaspoon sea salt
- ⅛ teaspoon freshly ground black pepper
- 4 eggs

1. Cook the beef. In a large deep skillet over medium-high heat, warm the olive oil. Add the beef and, stirring it occasionally, cook until it is completely browned, about 10 minutes. 2. Make the sauce. Add the bell pepper, zucchini, onion, and garlic to the skillet and sauté for 3 minutes. Stir in the tomato sauce, basil, oregano, salt, and pepper, bring it to a boil, and cook for about 10 minutes. 3. Cook the eggs. Make four wells in the beef mixture using the back of a spoon. Crack an egg into each well, then cover the skillet, reduce the heat to medium-low, and simmer until the eggs are cooked through, about 10 minutes. 4. Serve. Divide the mixture between four bowls, making sure to include an egg in each serving.

Per Serving:

calories: 275 | fat: 19g | protein: 18g | carbs: 8g | net carbs: 6g | fiber: 2g

All-Inclusive Bagels

Prep time: 15 minutes | Cook time: 14 minutes | Makes 6 bagels

- 1¾ cups shredded Mozzarella cheese or goat cheese Mozzarella
- 2 tablespoons unsalted butter or coconut oil
- 1 large egg, beaten
- 1 tablespoon apple cider
- vinegar
- 1 cup blanched almond flour
- 1 tablespoon baking powder
- ⅛ teaspoon fine sea salt
- 1½ teaspoons everything bagel seasoning

1. Make the dough: Put the Mozzarella and butter in a large microwave-safe bowl and microwave for 1 to 2 minutes, until the cheese is entirely melted. Stir well. Add the egg and vinegar. Using a hand mixer on medium, combine well. Add the almond flour, baking powder, and salt and, using the mixer, combine well. 2. Lay a piece of parchment paper on the countertop and place the dough on it. Knead it for about 3 minutes. The dough should be a little sticky but pliable. (If the dough is too sticky, chill it in the refrigerator for an hour or overnight.) 3. Preheat the air fryer to 350ºF (177ºC). Spray a baking sheet or pie pan that will fit into your air fryer with avocado oil. 4. Divide the dough into 6 equal portions. Roll 1 portion into a log that is 6 inches long and about ½ inch thick. Form the log into a circle and seal the edges together, making a bagel shape. Repeat with the remaining portions of dough, making 6 bagels. 5. Place the bagels on the greased baking sheet. Spray the bagels with avocado oil and top with everything bagel seasoning, pressing the seasoning into the dough with your hands. 6. Place the bagels in the air fryer and bake for 14 minutes, or until cooked through and golden brown, flipping after 6 minutes. 7. Remove the bagels from the air fryer and allow them to cool slightly before slicing them in half and serving. Store leftovers in an airtight container in the fridge for up to 4 days or in the freezer for up to a month.

Per Serving:

calories: 290 | fat: 25g | protein: 13g | carbs: 7g | net carbs: 4g | fiber: 3g

Tofu Scramble with Market Vegetables

Prep time: 10 minutes | Cook time: 10 minutes | serves 4

- 1 (14-ounce) block firm sprouted organic tofu, pressed and drained
- 2 tablespoons tahini
- 2 tablespoons nutritional yeast
- 1 tablespoon chia seeds
- ¼ teaspoon turmeric powder
- ⅛ teaspoon kala namak salt
- 2 tablespoons cold-pressed
- coconut oil
- ⅓ cup diced yellow onion
- ⅓ cup diced green bell pepper
- ¼ teaspoon garlic powder
- ¼ cup olives
- 2 cups coarsely chopped fresh spinach
- 1 teaspoon hot sauce (optional)

1. Blot the tofu with a paper towel to remove as much water as possible, then crumble it by hand into a large mixing bowl. 2. Add the tahini, nutritional yeast, chia seeds, turmeric, and kala namak salt to the bowl. Toss the ingredients together and set aside. 3. Heat the coconut oil in a large skillet over medium heat. 4. Add the onion, bell pepper, and garlic powder to the skillet. 5. Once the vegetables are tender and caramelized, toss in the olives and tofu mixture. 6. Allow the tofu to cook undisturbed for about 4 minutes to create a toasted, hash-like texture, then toss once to toast it a bit more. 7. Once the tofu is toasty, remove the skillet from the heat and stir in the spinach until it wilts. 8. Serve with your favorite hot sauce (if using).

Per Serving:

calories: 253 | fat: 18g | protein: 15g | carbs: 11g | net carbs: 7g | fiber: 4g

Creamy Mushroom and Cheese Lettuce Wraps

Prep time: 10 minutes | Cook time: 10 minutes | Serves 4

For the Wraps:

+ 6 eggs
+ 2 tablespoons almond milk

For the Filling:

+ 1 teaspoon olive oil
+ 1 cup mushrooms, chopped
+ Salt and black pepper, to taste
+ ½ teaspoon cayenne pepper

+ 1 tablespoon olive oil
+ Sea salt, to taste

+ 8 fresh lettuce leaves
+ 4 slices gruyere cheese
+ 2 tomatoes, sliced

1. Mix all the ingredients for the wraps thoroughly. 2. Set a frying pan over medium heat. Add in ¼ of the mixture and cook for 4 minutes on both sides. Do the same thrice and set the wraps aside, they should be kept warm. 3. In a separate pan over medium heat, warm 1 teaspoon of olive oil. Cook the mushrooms for 5 minutes until soft; add cayenne pepper, black pepper, and salt. Set 1-2 lettuce leaves onto every wrap, split the mushrooms among the wraps and top with tomatoes and cheese.

Per Serving:

calories: 273 | fat: 20g | protein: 18g | carbs: 5g | net carbs: 4g | fiber: 1g

Hearty Sausage, Spinach, and Goat Cheese Bake

Prep time: 10 minutes | Cook time: 40 minutes | Makes 10 squares

+ Butter or coconut oil, for greasing
+ 1 pound (454 g) breakfast sausage or ground pork
+ 1 (10-ounce / 283-g) package frozen spinach, thawed and squeezed to remove excess liquid
+ 12 eggs

+ ½ cup heavy (whipping) cream
+ 1 teaspoon sea salt
+ ½ teaspoon freshly ground black pepper
+ 5 ounces (142 g) goat cheese, crumbled

1. Preheat the oven to 400ºF (205ºC) and grease a 9-by-13-inch baking dish. 2. In a medium bowl, break up the sausage into small pieces. Add the spinach and mix well. Spread the mixture over the bottom of the prepared baking dish. 3. In a large bowl, whisk together the eggs, cream, salt, and pepper. Slowly pour the egg mixture over the sausage and spinach and then top with the cheese. 4. Bake for 30 to 40 minutes until fluffy and set. 5. Let cool and then cut into 10 squares. Refrigerate portions for the week in a glass container or resealable plastic bag and freeze the rest for up to 3 months. To serve, reheat in the microwave for 1 minute if previously thawed in the refrigerator overnight or 2 minutes if frozen.

Per Serving:

1 square: calories: 322 | fat: 26g | protein: 19g | carbs: 3g | net carbs: 2g | fiber: 1g

Smoky Flavored Sausage Patties

- 1 pound (454 g) ground pork
- 1 tablespoon coconut aminos
- 2 teaspoons liquid smoke
- 1 teaspoon dried sage
- 1 teaspoon sea salt
- ½ teaspoon fennel seeds
- ½ teaspoon dried thyme
- ½ teaspoon freshly ground black pepper
- ¼ teaspoon cayenne pepper

1. In a large bowl, combine the pork, coconut aminos, liquid smoke, sage, salt, fennel seeds, thyme, black pepper, and cayenne pepper. Work the meat with your hands until the seasonings are fully incorporated. 2. Shape the mixture into 8 equal-size patties. Using your thumb, make a dent in the center of each patty. Place the patties on a plate and cover with plastic wrap. Refrigerate the patties for at least 30 minutes. 3. Working in batches if necessary, place the patties in a single layer in the air fryer, being careful not to overcrowd them. 4. Set the air fryer to 400ºF (204ºC) and air fry for 5 minutes. Flip and cook for about 4 minutes more.

Per Serving:

calories: 177 | fat: 13g | protein: 13g | carbs: 2g | net carbs: 1g | fiber: 1g

Pork and Quill Egg Bites

- 10 ounces (283 g) ground pork
- 1 jalapeño pepper, chopped
- 1 tablespoon butter, softened
- 1 teaspoon dried dill
- ½ teaspoon salt
- 1 cup water
- 4 quill eggs

1. In a bowl, stir together all the ingredients, except for the quill eggs and water. Transfer the meat mixture to the silicone muffin molds and press the surface gently. 2. Pour the water and insert the trivet in the Instant Pot. Put the meat cups on the trivet. 3. Crack the eggs over the meat mixture. 4. Set the lid in place. Select the Manual mode and set the cooking time for 15 minutes on High Pressure. When the timer goes off, do a quick pressure release. Carefully open the lid. 5. Serve warm.

Per Serving:

calories: 142 | fat: 6g | protein: 20g | carbs: 0g | net carbs: 0g | fiber: 0g

Low-Carb English Muffins

- 1 teaspoon coconut oil, for greasing the ramekin
- 1 large egg
- 2 teaspoons coconut flour
- Pinch of baking soda
- Pinch of fine sea salt

1. Grease a 4-ounce (113-g) ramekin with the coconut oil. If using the toaster oven method, preheat the toaster oven to 400ºF (205ºC). 2. In a small mixing bowl, combine the egg and coconut flour with a fork until well combined, then add the rest of the ingredients and stir to combine. 3. Place the dough in the greased ramekin. To cook in a microwave, cook on high for 1 minute, until a toothpick inserted in the middle comes out clean. To cook in a toaster oven, bake for 12 minutes, until a toothpick inserted in the middle comes out clean. 4. Allow to cool in the ramekin for 5 minutes. Remove the muffin from the ramekin and allow to cool completely. Slice in half and serve.

Per Serving:

calories: 130 | fat: 7g | protein: 8g | carbs: 8g | net carbs: 3g | fiber: 5g

Chapter 3

Poultry

Chipotle Drumsticks

Prep time: 5 minutes | Cook time: 25 minutes | Serves 4

- 1 tablespoon tomato paste
- ½ teaspoon chipotle powder
- ¼ teaspoon apple cider vinegar
- ¼ teaspoon garlic powder
- 8 chicken drumsticks
- ½ teaspoon salt
- ⅛ teaspoon ground black pepper

1. In a small bowl, combine the tomato paste, chipotle powder, vinegar, and garlic powder. Mix well until all ingredients are thoroughly combined. 2. Season the drumsticks with salt and pepper, then place them in a large bowl. Pour the tomato paste mixture over the drumsticks and toss or stir to ensure that all the drumsticks are evenly coated in the mixture. 3. Place the coated drumsticks into the ungreased basket of the air fryer. Set the temperature to 400ºF (204ºC) and air fry for 25 minutes, turning the drumsticks halfway through the cooking time for even cooking. The drumsticks should be dark red and have an internal temperature of at least 165ºF (74ºC) when fully cooked. 4. Once done, remove the drumsticks from the air fryer and serve warm. Enjoy your flavorful chipotle drumsticks!

Per Serving:
calories: 257 | fat: 14g | protein: 31g | carbs: 3g | net carbs: 2g | fiber: 1g

Braised Chicken with Olives

Prep time: 10 minutes | Cook time: 45 minutes | Serves 6

- 6 bone-in, skin-on chicken thighs (approximately 2 pounds / 907 g)
- 2 teaspoons kosher salt
- Freshly ground black pepper, to taste
- 3 tablespoons avocado oil, or more as needed
- 1 small onion, halved and thinly sliced (approximately ½ cup)
- 4 garlic cloves, chopped
- 2 teaspoons ground cumin
- 1 teaspoon smoked paprika
- 1 teaspoon ground ginger
- 1 teaspoon ground cinnamon, or 2 cinnamon sticks (optional)
- 2 cups chicken broth, preferably homemade
- 1 dried bay leaf
- 2 lemons, preferably Meyer lemons
- 1 cup pitted olives

1. Sprinkle 1 teaspoon of salt and some pepper on the tops of the chicken thighs. In a large skillet, heat the oil over medium-high heat until it reaches a high temperature. Carefully place the chicken skin side down into the hot oil and allow it to cook undisturbed for 3 to 5 minutes. Season the chicken with additional salt and pepper, then turn it over to sear the other side for approximately another 3 minutes. 2. Transfer the chicken to a plate. If the skillet appears too dry, add a bit more oil and lower the heat to medium. Introduce the onion and sauté for about 5 minutes until it becomes tender. Add the garlic and continue to sauté for 1 minute. Incorporate the cumin, paprika, and ginger, along with the ground cinnamon if desired, stirring thoroughly. (If you are using cinnamon sticks, add them later in the process.) 3. Gradually pour in the broth, making sure to scrape up any browned bits from the bottom of the pan. Increase the heat to medium-high, return the chicken to the skillet, and pour any juices that have accumulated on the plate back into the pan. Add the bay leaf and cinnamon sticks, if using, to the broth. 4. Cut one of the lemons into wedges and tuck those wedges among the chicken thighs. Evenly distribute the olives over the chicken. Squeeze the juice from the remaining lemon over the entire dish. 5. Bring the liquid to a boil, then reduce the heat to a gentle simmer. Cover the skillet and let it simmer for 30 minutes. Remove the bay leaf and cinnamon sticks before serving. Plate the chicken thighs and generously spoon the sauce from the pan over them.

Per Serving:
calories: 368 | fat: 26g | protein: 27g | carbs: 7g | net carbs: 5g | fiber: 2g

Cheese Stuffed Chicken

Prep time: 15 minutes | Cook time: 20 minutes | Serves 4

- 12 ounces (340 g) chicken fillet
- 4 ounces (113 g) provolone cheese, sliced
- 1 tablespoon cream cheese
- ½ teaspoon dried cilantro
- ½ teaspoon smoked paprika
- 1 cup water, for cooking

1. Begin by beating the chicken fillet until it is an even thickness. Rub the fillet with dried cilantro and smoked paprika to season it well. 2. Spread a layer of cream cheese over the seasoned chicken, then top it with slices of Provolone cheese. 3. Carefully roll the chicken fillet into a tight roll and wrap it securely in aluminum foil. 4. Pour 1 cup of water into the Instant Pot and insert the rack (trivet) into the pot. 5. Place the wrapped chicken roll on the rack inside the Instant Pot. Close the lid and seal the vent. 6. Set the Instant Pot to Manual mode and cook on High Pressure for 20 minutes. 7. Once the cooking time is complete, perform a quick pressure release to release the steam. Carefully remove the chicken roll from the pot, unwrap it from the foil, and slice it into servings. Enjoy your delicious stuffed chicken roll!

Per Serving:
calories: 271 | fat: 15g | protein: 32g | carbs: 1g | net carbs: 1g | fiber: 0g

Chicken and Zucchini Bake

Prep time: 10 minutes | Cook time: 30 minutes | Serves 4

- 1 zucchini, chopped
- Salt and black pepper, to taste
- 1 teaspoon garlic powder
- 1 tablespoon avocado oil
- 2chicken breasts, skinless, boneless, sliced
- 1 tomato, cored and chopped
- ½ teaspoon dried oregano
- ½ teaspoon dried basil
- ½ cup mozzarella cheese, shredded

1. Season the chicken with pepper, garlic powder, and salt. Heat avocado oil in a pan over medium heat, then add the chicken slices and cook until they turn golden brown; transfer them to a baking dish. In the same pan, toss in the zucchini, tomato, pepper, basil, oregano, and a pinch of salt, cooking for 2 minutes before spreading the mixture over the chicken. 2. Place the dish in the oven and bake at 330ºF for 20 minutes. Afterward, sprinkle mozzarella cheese over the chicken, return it to the oven, and bake for an additional 5 minutes, or until the cheese is melted and bubbly. Serve alongside a fresh green salad.

Per Serving:

calories: 279 | fat: 15g | protein: 33g | carbs: 3g | net carbs: 2g | fiber: 1g

Thai Tacos with Peanut Sauce

Prep time: 10 minutes | Cook time: 6 minutes | Serves 4

- 1 pound (454 g) ground chicken
- ¼ cup diced onions (about 1 small onion)
- 2 cloves garlic, minced
- ¼ teaspoon fine sea salt

Sauce:

- ¼ cup creamy peanut butter, room temperature
- 2 tablespoons chicken broth, plus more if needed
- 2 tablespoons lime juice
- 2 tablespoons grated fresh ginger
- 2 tablespoons wheat-free tamari or coconut aminos
- 1½ teaspoons hot sauce
- 5 drops liquid stevia (optional)

For Serving:

- 2 small heads butter lettuce, leaves separated
- Lime slices (optional)

For Garnish (Optional):

- Cilantro leaves
- Shredded purple cabbage
- Sliced green onions

1. Preheat the air fryer to 350ºF (177ºC). 2. In a pie pan or a dish that fits in your air fryer, combine the ground chicken, chopped onions, minced garlic, and salt. Use a spatula to break up the chicken. Place the dish in the air fryer and cook for 5 minutes, or until the chicken is browned and cooked through. After cooking, break up the chicken into small crumbles. 3. To make the sauce, in a medium-sized bowl, stir together the peanut butter, broth, lime juice, grated ginger, tamari, hot sauce, and stevia (if using) until well combined. If the sauce is too thick, add an additional tablespoon or two of broth. Taste and adjust the hot sauce to your preference. 4. Add half of the sauce to the pan with the cooked chicken. Cook for another minute, stirring well to combine and heat through. 5. To assemble the tacos, place several lettuce leaves on a serving plate. Spoon a few tablespoons of the chicken mixture into each lettuce leaf and garnish with cilantro leaves, shredded purple cabbage, and sliced green onions, if desired. Serve the remaining sauce on the side, along with lime slices if you like. 6. Store any leftover chicken mixture in an airtight container in the refrigerator for up to 4 days. Keep the leftover sauce, lettuce leaves, and garnishes stored separately. To reheat the meat mixture, place it in a lightly greased pie pan in the preheated air fryer at 350ºF (177ºC) for 3 minutes, or until heated through. Enjoy your delicious chicken lettuce tacos!

Per Serving:

calories: 276 | fat: 18g | protein: 25g | carbs: 5g | net carbs: 4g | fiber: 1g

Parmesan-Crusted Chicken

Prep time: 15 minutes | Cook time: 13 minutes | Serves 2

- 1 tomato, sliced
- 8 ounces (227 g) chicken fillets
- 2 ounces (57 g) Parmesan, sliced
- 1 teaspoon butter
- 4 tablespoons water, for sprinkling
- 1 cup water, for cooking

1. Add water to the instant pot and place the steamer rack inside. 2. Next, grease the baking mold with a layer of butter. 3. Cut the chicken fillets in half and arrange them in the mold. 4. Drizzle some water over the chicken and layer it with tomato slices and Parmesan cheese. 5. Cover the baking mold with aluminum foil and set it on the rack. 6. Securely close and seal the lid of the instant pot. 7. Set the cooking mode to Manual and cook for 13 minutes. Afterward, let the pressure release naturally for 10 minutes.

Per Serving:

calories: 329 | fat: 16g | protein: 42g | carbs: 2g | net carbs: 2g | fiber: 0g

Shredded Chicken

Prep time: 5 minutes | Cook time: 14 minutes | Serves 4

- ½ teaspoon salt
- ½ teaspoon pepper
- ½ teaspoon dried oregano
- ½ teaspoon dried basil
- ½ teaspoon garlic powder
- 2 (6-ounce / 170-g) boneless, skinless chicken breasts
- 1 tablespoon coconut oil
- 1 cup water

1. In a small bowl, combine the salt, pepper, oregano, basil, and garlic powder. Rub this seasoning mix over both sides of the chicken to ensure it is well coated. 2. Set your Instant Pot to the Sauté function and heat the coconut oil until it is sizzling. 3. Add the seasoned chicken to the pot and sear for 3 to 4 minutes on each side, or until golden brown. 4. Once seared, remove the chicken from the pot and set it aside. 5. Pour the water into the Instant Pot, using a wooden spoon or rubber spatula to scrape up any seasoning that may be stuck to the bottom of the pot. This helps prevent the burn notice. 6. Place the trivet into the Instant Pot and set the seared chicken on top of the trivet. 7. Secure the lid on the Instant Pot. Select the Manual mode and set the cooking time for 10 minutes at High Pressure. 8. After the cooking time is complete, allow for a natural pressure release for 5 minutes, then carefully release any remaining pressure. Open the lid cautiously. 9. Remove the chicken from the pot and shred it using two forks. Serve the shredded chicken as desired. Enjoy your deliciously seasoned chicken!

Per Serving:
calories: 135 | fat: 5g | protein: 20g | carbs: 0g | net carbs: 0g | fiber: 0g

Zesty Grilled Chicken

Prep time: 5 minutes | Cook time: 20 minutes | Serves 8

- 2½ pounds chicken thighs and drumsticks
- 1 tablespoon coconut aminos
- 1 tablespoon apple cider vinegar
- A pinch of red pepper flakes
- Salt and black pepper, to taste
- ½ teaspoonground ginger
- ⅓ cup butter
- 1 garlic clove, minced
- 1 teaspoon lime zest
- ½ cup warm water

1. In a blender, combine the butter, water, salt, ginger, vinegar, garlic, pepper, lime zest, aminos, and red pepper flakes. Blend until smooth. Pat the chicken dry and place it on a pan. Pour the zesty marinade over the chicken, ensuring it is well coated. Cover

and refrigerate for 1 hour to allow the flavors to meld. 2. Preheat your grill to medium heat. Place the chicken pieces skin side down on the grill and cook for 10 minutes. After 10 minutes, turn the chicken, brush it with some of the reserved marinade, and cook for an additional 10 minutes, or until the chicken is fully cooked and has nice grill marks. Once done, split the chicken among serving plates and enjoy!

Per Serving:
calories: 286 | fat: 14g | protein: 37g | carbs: 3g | net carbs: 3g | fiber: 0g

Turkey Meatloaf Florentine Muffins

Prep time: 10 minutes | Cook time: 25 minutes | Serves 6

- ½ pound (227 g) frozen spinach, thawed
- 2 pounds (907 g) ground turkey
- ½ cup (2 ounces / 57 g) blanched almond flour
- 2 large eggs
- 4 cloves garlic, minced
- 2 teaspoons sea salt
- ½ teaspoon black pepper
- 2¼ cups (9 ounces / 255 g) shredded Mozzarella cheese, divided into 1½ cups (6 ounces / 170 g) and ¾ cup (3 ounces / 85 g)
- ⅓ cup no-sugar-added marinara sauce

1. Preheat the oven to 375ºF (190ºC). Lightly grease 12 cups of a muffin tin and place it on top of a sheet pan for easier cleanup. 2. Drain the spinach and squeeze it tightly in a kitchen towel to remove as much water as possible. 3. In a large bowl, combine the drained spinach, ground turkey, almond flour, eggs, minced garlic, sea salt, and black pepper. Mix until just combined, being careful not to overwork the meat. 4. Fill each muffin cup with 2 tablespoons of the turkey mixture. Use the back of a measuring spoon or your hands to create a well in the center of each cup. Pack each well with 2 tablespoons of mozzarella cheese (totaling 1½ cups or 6 ounces / 170 g). Top each well with an additional 2 tablespoons of the turkey mixture, lightly pressing down along the sides to seal the filling inside. 5. Spread 1 teaspoon of marinara sauce over each meatloaf muffin and sprinkle with another 1 tablespoon of mozzarella cheese (totaling ¾ cup or 3 ounces / 85 g). 6. Bake in the preheated oven for 20 to 25 minutes, or until the internal temperature reaches at least 160ºF (71ºC). Allow the muffins to rest for 5 minutes before serving, as the temperature will rise another 5 degrees while resting. Enjoy your delicious spinach and turkey meatloaf muffins!

Per Serving:
calories: 380 | fat: 16g | protein: 52g | carbs: 6g | net carbs: 4g | fiber: 2g

Thyme Chicken Thighs

Prep time: 5 minutes | Cook time: 15 minutes | Serves 4

- ½ cup chicken stock
- 1 tablespoon olive oil
- ½ cup chopped onion
- 4 chicken thighs
- ¼ cup heavy cream
- 2 tablespoons Dijon mustard
- 1 teaspoon thyme
- 1 teaspoon garlic powder

1. Heat the olive oil in a pan over medium heat. Add the chicken and cook for about 4 minutes on each side, or until it is golden brown and cooked through. Once done, set the chicken aside on a plate. 2. In the same pan, add the chopped onion and sauté for about 3 minutes, or until it becomes translucent. 3. Pour in the chicken stock and bring it to a simmer. Let it simmer for about 5 minutes to allow the flavors to meld. 4. Stir in the mustard and heavy cream, followed by the thyme and garlic powder. Mix well until the sauce is smooth and heated through. 5. Pour the creamy sauce over the cooked chicken. Serve immediately, garnished with additional thyme if desired. Enjoy your delicious chicken with creamy mustard sauce!

Per Serving:
calories: 321 | fat: 23g | protein: 19g | carbs: 5g | net carbs: 4g | fiber: 1g

Ethiopian Chicken with Cauliflower

Prep time: 15 minutes | Cook time: 28 minutes | Serves 6

- 2 handful fresh Italian parsley, roughly chopped
- ½ cup fresh chopped chives
- 2 sprigs thyme
- 6 chicken drumsticks
- 1½ small-sized head cauliflower, broken into large-sized florets
- 2 teaspoons mustard powder
- ⅓ teaspoon porcini powder
- 1½ teaspoons berbere spice
- ⅓ teaspoon sweet paprika
- ½ teaspoon shallot powder
- 1 teaspoon granulated garlic
- 1 teaspoon freshly cracked pink peppercorns
- ½ teaspoon sea salt

1. In a bowl, combine all the ingredients for the berbere spice rub mix. Once mixed, coat the chicken drumsticks thoroughly with the rub on all sides. Place the seasoned drumsticks in a baking dish. 2. Next, arrange the cauliflower florets on top of the chicken drumsticks. Sprinkle with thyme, chives, and Italian parsley, then lightly spritz everything with pan spray. Transfer the baking dish to the preheated air fryer. 3. Set the timer for 28 minutes and roast at 355°F (179°C), turning the drumsticks and cauliflower occasionally

for even cooking. Bon appétit!

Per Serving:
calories: 235 | fat: 12g | protein: 25g | carbs: 5g | net carbs: 3g | fiber: 2g

Chicken Fajitas

Prep time: 10 minutes | Cook time: 15 to 20 minutes | Serves 4

- 1 pound (454 g) boneless, skinless chicken breasts and/or thighs, sliced into thin strips
- 1 teaspoon salt
- 1 teaspoon dried oregano
- 1 teaspoon garlic powder
- ½ teaspoon freshly ground black pepper
- 1 teaspoon ground cumin
- ½ teaspoon red pepper flakes
- ½ teaspoon paprika
- ¼ teaspoon ground cinnamon
- 2 tablespoons avocado oil
- or butter, divided
- ½ white onion, sliced
- ½ red bell pepper, sliced into strips
- ½ green bell pepper, sliced into strips
- 2 tablespoons chicken broth (optional)
- 2 to 4 coconut or almond flour wraps, or grain-free chips
- 1 cup shredded romaine lettuce
- Sugar-free salsa, guacamole, sour cream, and shredded cheese, for serving (optional)

1. In a large bowl, combine the chicken with salt, oregano, garlic powder, pepper, cumin, red pepper flakes, paprika, cinnamon, and 1 tablespoon of oil or butter. Mix well to ensure the chicken is evenly coated with the spices. 2. Heat the remaining tablespoon of oil or butter in a large, shallow skillet over medium-high heat. Add the chopped onion and cook for 3 to 5 minutes, stirring occasionally, until the onion becomes translucent. 3. Add the bell peppers to the skillet and continue to cook, stirring frequently, for another 5 minutes, or until the peppers are tender. 4. Add the seasoned chicken mixture to the skillet and cook, stirring, for an additional 2 to 3 minutes. Then, reduce the heat to medium, cover the skillet, and cook for about 5 minutes, or until the chicken is cooked through and no longer pink. If the chicken starts to burn, add a splash of chicken broth to prevent sticking. 5. Once cooked, remove the chicken mixture from the heat and let it cool slightly. 6. To serve, divide the wraps or chips among plates. Sprinkle shredded romaine lettuce on top, then spoon the chicken fajita mixture over the lettuce. Serve the fajitas with salsa, guacamole, sour cream, and cheese, if desired. Enjoy your delicious chicken fajitas!

Per Serving:
calories: 235 | fat: 13g | protein: 25g | carbs: 5g | net carbs: 3g | fiber: 2g

Stuffed Chicken with Spinach and Feta

Prep time: 10 minutes | Cook time: 25 minutes | Serves 4

- ½ cup frozen spinach
- ⅓ cup crumbled feta cheese
- 1¼ teaspoons salt, divided
- 4 (6-ounce / 170-g) boneless, skinless chicken breasts, butterflied
- ¼ teaspoon pepper
- ¼ teaspoon dried oregano
- ¼ teaspoon dried parsley
- ¼ teaspoon garlic powder
- 2 tablespoons coconut oil
- 1 cup water

1. In a medium bowl, combine the spinach, feta cheese, and ¼ teaspoon of salt. Mix well. Divide the mixture evenly and spoon it onto the chicken breasts. 2. Close the chicken breasts around the filling and secure them with toothpicks or butcher's string to keep the filling inside. Sprinkle the chicken with the remaining 1 teaspoon of salt, along with pepper, oregano, parsley, and garlic powder for added flavor. 3. Set your Instant Pot to the Sauté function and heat the coconut oil until hot. 4. Sear each chicken breast in the pot until golden brown, about 4 to 5 minutes per side. 5. Once browned, remove the chicken breasts from the pot and set them aside. 6. Pour the water into the Instant Pot, using a wooden spoon to scrape the bottom and remove any bits of chicken or seasoning that may be stuck. Add the trivet to the pot and place the seared chicken on top of the trivet. 7. Secure the lid on the Instant Pot. Select the Manual mode and set the cooking time for 15 minutes at High Pressure. 8. Once the cooking time is complete, allow for a natural pressure release for 15 minutes, then carefully release any remaining pressure. Open the lid cautiously. Serve the stuffed chicken breasts warm, and enjoy your delicious meal!

Per Serving:

calories: 303 | fat: 12g | protein: 41g | carbs: 1g | net carbs: 1g | fiber: 1g

Spice-Rubbed Chicken Thighs

Prep time: 10 minutes | Cook time: 25 minutes | Serves 4

- 4 (4-ounce / 113-g) bone-in, skin-on chicken thighs
- ½ teaspoon salt
- ½ teaspoon garlic powder
- 2 teaspoons chili powder
- 1 teaspoon paprika
- 1 teaspoon ground cumin
- 1 small lime, halved

1. Pat the chicken thighs dry with paper towels and sprinkle them evenly with salt, garlic powder, chili powder, paprika, and cumin. Make sure to coat them well for maximum flavor. 2. Squeeze the juice from ½ lime over the seasoned thighs, ensuring they are well-coated. Place the thighs into the ungreased air fryer basket in a single layer. 3. Adjust the air fryer temperature to 380ºF (193ºC) and roast the chicken thighs for 25 minutes, turning them halfway through the cooking time to ensure even crispiness. The thighs should be crispy and browned, with an internal temperature of at least 165ºF (74ºC) when done. 4. Once cooked, transfer the thighs to a large serving plate and drizzle with the remaining lime juice for added flavor. Serve warm and enjoy your delicious, crispy chicken thighs!

Per Serving:

calories: 248 | fat: 17g | protein: 21g | carbs: 2g | net carbs: 1g | fiber: 1g

Chicken and Scallions Stuffed Peppers

Prep time: 5 minutes | Cook time: 20 minutes | Serves 5

- 1 tablespoon butter, at room temperature
- ½ cup scallions, chopped
- 1 pound (454 g) ground chicken
- ½ teaspoon sea salt
- ½ teaspoon chili powder
- ⅓ teaspoon paprika
- ⅓ teaspoon ground cumin
- ¼ teaspoon shallot powder
- 6 ounces (170 g) goat cheese, crumbled
- 1½ cups water
- 5 bell peppers, tops, membrane, and seeds removed
- ½ cup sour cream

1. Set your Instant Pot to the Sauté function and melt the butter. 2. Add the chopped scallions and chicken to the pot, sautéing for 2 to 3 minutes until the chicken is lightly browned. 3. Stir in the sea salt, chili powder, paprika, cumin, and shallot powder. Add the crumbled goat cheese and mix well. Once combined, transfer the mixture to a bowl and set aside. 4. Clean the Instant Pot by removing any residue. Pour the water into the pot and insert the trivet. 5. Take the bell peppers and stuff them with enough of the chicken mixture, being careful not to pack them too tightly. Place the stuffed peppers on the trivet in the Instant Pot. 6. Lock the lid in place. Select the Poultry mode and set the cooking time for 15 minutes at High Pressure. 7. When the timer beeps, allow for a natural pressure release for 10 minutes, then carefully release any remaining pressure. Open the lid cautiously. 8. Remove the stuffed peppers from the Instant Pot and serve with sour cream on the side. Enjoy your delicious stuffed bell peppers!

Per Serving:

calories: 338 | fat: 20g | protein: 30g | carbs: 9g | net carbs: 7g | fiber: 1g

Dijon Turkey

- 14 ounces (397 g) ground turkey
- 1 tablespoon Dijon mustard
- ½ cup coconut flour
- 1 teaspoon onion powder
- 1 teaspoon salt
- ½ cup chicken broth
- 1 tablespoon avocado oil

1. In a mixing bowl, combine ground turkey, Dijon mustard, coconut flour, onion powder, and salt. Mix well until all ingredients are thoroughly incorporated. 2. Using your fingertips, shape the mixture into meatballs of your desired size. 3. Pour avocado oil into the Instant Pot and heat it for 1 minute on the sauté setting. 4. Add the meatballs to the pot and cook for 2 minutes on each side until they are browned. 5. Once browned, pour in the chicken broth. Close and seal the lid of the Instant Pot. 6. Set the Instant Pot to cook the meatballs for 10 minutes. After the cooking time is complete, perform a quick pressure release to release the steam. Enjoy your delicious meatballs!

Per Serving:
calories: 268 | fat: 13g | protein: 30g | carbs: 11g | net carbs: 5g | fiber: 6g

Caprese Chicken Skillet

- 1 tablespoon extra-virgin olive oil
- 1 pound boneless, skinless chicken thighs
- 1½ teaspoons pink Himalayan salt, divided
- ½ teaspoon ground black pepper
- 1 teaspoon minced garlic
- 12 cherry tomatoes, halved (about 3 ounces)
- ¼ teaspoon red pepper flakes
- 1 medium-sized zucchini, spiral-sliced into noodles
- 3 or 4 large fresh basil leaves, minced
- 3 ounces mini mozzarella balls, halved

1. In a large skillet, heat the olive oil over medium-high heat. 2. Chop the chicken into 1-inch pieces and season with 1 teaspoon of salt and black pepper. 3. Add the seasoned chicken to the hot skillet and cook for 5 to 7 minutes, or until fully cooked and no longer pink in the center. Once cooked, remove the chicken from the skillet and set it aside. 4. Lower the heat to low and use a spatula to scrape up any drippings from the bottom of the skillet. Add the garlic and sauté for about 20 seconds. Then, add the tomatoes, the remaining ½ teaspoon of salt, and red pepper flakes. Stir to combine, cover with a lid, and cook for 5 to 7 minutes, until the tomatoes have burst and softened. 5. Increase the heat back to high, add the zucchini noodles and basil, and cook for 1 minute, until the noodles are slightly tender but still firm. Remove from heat, add the cooked chicken and mozzarella, and toss everything together to combine. Serve immediately.

Per Serving:
calories: 226 | fat: 12g | protein: 26g | carbs: 4g | net carbs: 3g | fiber: 1g

Chili Lime Turkey Burgers

Burgers:

- 2 pounds (907 g) ground turkey
- 1½ ounces (43 g) diced red onion
- 2 cloves garlic, minced
- 1½ teaspoons minced

- cilantro
- 1½ teaspoons salt
- 1 teaspoon Mexican chili powder
- Juice and zest of 1 lime
- ½ cup water

Dipping Sauce:

- ½ cup sour cream
- 4 teaspoons sriracha
- 1 tablespoon chopped

- cilantro, plus more for garnish
- 1 teaspoon lime juice

1. To make the burgers, in a large bowl, combine the ground turkey, chopped onion, minced garlic, chopped cilantro, salt, chili powder, and lime juice and zest. Use a wooden spoon to mix until all ingredients are well distributed. 2. Divide the mixture into four equal portions, each weighing 8 ounces (227 g). Shape each portion into thick patties, about 1 inch thick. 3. Add 1 cup of water and the trivet to the Instant Pot. Place the turkey patties on top of the trivet, overlapping them if necessary. 4. Close the lid of the Instant Pot and seal the vent. Cook on High Pressure for 3 minutes. Once the cooking time is complete, perform a quick release to release the steam. 5. Carefully remove the patties from the pot and set them aside. 6. To make the dipping sauce, in a small bowl, whisk together the sour cream, sriracha, chopped cilantro, and lime juice until well combined. 7. Top each turkey patty with 2 tablespoons of the dipping sauce and garnish with fresh cilantro. Serve and enjoy your flavorful turkey burgers!

Per Serving:
calories: 417 | fat: 25g | protein: 44g | carbs: 5g | net carbs: 4g | fiber: 1g

Chapter **4**

Beef, Pork, and Lamb

Beef Steak Topped with Cheesy Mushroom Sauce

- 1 tablespoon olive oil
- 1½ pounds (680 g) beef blade steak
- 1 cup stock
- 2 garlic cloves, minced

Sauce:
- 1 tablespoon butter, softened
- 2 cups sliced Porcini mushrooms
- ½ cup thinly sliced onions
- Sea salt and ground black pepper, to taste
- ½ teaspoon cayenne pepper
- 1 tablespoon coconut aminos
- ½ cup sour cream
- 4 ounces (113 g) goat cheese, crumbled

1. Press the Sauté button to heat up the Instant Pot. Then, heat the olive oil until sizzling. Once hot, cook the blade steak approximately 3 minutes or until delicately browned. 2. Add the stock, garlic, salt, black pepper, cayenne pepper, and coconut aminos. 3. Secure the lid. Choose Manual mode and High Pressure; cook for 20 minutes. Once cooking is complete, use a quick pressure release; carefully remove the lid. 4. Take the meat out of the Instant Pot. Allow it to cool slightly and then, slice it into strips. 5. Press the Sauté button again and add the butter, mushrooms and onions to the Instant Pot. Let it cook for 5 minutes longer or until the mushrooms are fragrant and the onions are softened. 6. Add sour cream and goat cheese; continue to simmer for a couple of minutes more or until everything is thoroughly heated. 7. Return the meat to the Instant Pot and serve. Bon appétit!

Per Serving:
calories: 311 | fat: 20g | protein: 31g | carbs: 3g | net carbs: 3g | fiber: 0g

Crispy Golden Bacon Strips

- 6 ounces (170 g) bacon, sliced
- 2 tablespoons almond flour
- 1 tablespoon water
- ¾ teaspoon chili pepper

1. Sprinkle the sliced bacon with the almond flour and drizzle with water. Add the chili pepper. 2. Put the bacon in the Instant Pot. 3. Cook on Sauté mode for 3 minutes per side. Serve immediately.

Per Serving:
calories: 251 | fat: 19g | protein: 17g | carbs: 2g | net carbs: 1g | fiber: 0g

Savory Beef Sausage Meat Loaf

- 1½ pounds Italian sausage meat
- 1 pound grass-fed ground beef
- ½ cup almond flour
- ¼ cup heavy (whipping) cream
- 1 egg, lightly beaten
- ½ onion, finely chopped
- ½ red bell pepper, chopped
- 2 teaspoons minced garlic
- 1 teaspoon dried oregano
- ¼ teaspoon sea salt
- ⅛ teaspoon freshly ground black pepper

1. Preheat the oven. Set the oven temperature to 400°F. 2. Make the meat loaf. In a large bowl, mix together the sausage, ground beef, almond flour, cream, egg, onion, red bell pepper, garlic, oregano, salt, and pepper until everything is well combined. Press the mixture into a 9-inch loaf pan. 3. Bake. Bake for 1 hour to 1 hour and 15 minutes, or until the meat loaf is cooked through. Drain off and throw out any grease and let the meat loaf stand for 10 minutes. 4. Serve. Cut the meat loaf into six slices, divide them between six plates, and serve it immediately.

Per Serving:
calories: 394 | fat: 34g | protein: 19g | carbs: 1g | net carbs: 1g | fiber: 0g

Zesty Mustard Lamb Chops

- Oil, for spraying
- 1 tablespoon Dijon mustard
- 2 teaspoons lemon juice
- ½ teaspoon dried tarragon
- ¼ teaspoon salt
- ¼ teaspoon freshly ground black pepper
- 4 (1¼-inch-thick) loin lamb chops

1. Preheat the air fryer to 390°F (199°C). Line the air fryer basket with parchment and spray lightly with oil. 2. In a small bowl, mix together the mustard, lemon juice, tarragon, salt, and black pepper. 3. Pat dry the lamb chops with a paper towel. Brush the chops on both sides with the mustard mixture. 4. Place the chops in the prepared basket. You may need to work in batches, depending on the size of your air fryer. 5. Cook for 8 minutes, flip, and cook for another 6 minutes, or until the internal temperature reaches 125°F (52°C) for rare, 145°F (63°C) for medium-rare, or 155°F (68°C) for medium.

Per Serving:
calories: 244 | fat: 13g | protein: 27g | carbs: 1g | net carbs: 1g | fiber: 0g

Beef Tripe Stir-Fried with Vegetables

Prep time: 10 minutes | Cook time: 23 minutes | Serves 6

- 1½ pounds beef tripe
- 4 cups buttermilk
- Salt to taste
- 2 teaspoons creole seasoning
- 3 tablespoons olive oil
- 2 large onions, sliced
- 3 tomatoes, diced

1. Put the tripe in a bowl and cover with buttermilk. Refrigerate for 3 hours to extract bitterness and gamey taste. Remove from buttermilk, pat dry with a paper towel, and season with salt and creole seasoning. 2. Heat 2 tbsp of oil in a skillet over medium heat and brown the tripe on both sides for 6 minutes in total. Set aside. Add the remaining oil and sauté the onions for 3 minutes until soft. Include the tomatoes and cook for 10 minutes. Pour in a few tablespoons of water if necessary. Put the tripe in the sauce and cook for 3 minutes. Adjust taste with salt and serve with low carb rice.

Per Serving:

calories: 314 | fat: 15g | protein: 26g | carbs: 18g | net carbs: 16g | fiber: 2g

Fiery Spiced Lamb Sirloin Chops

Prep time: 30 minutes | Cook time: 15 minutes | Serves 4

- ½ yellow onion, coarsely chopped
- 4 coin-size slices peeled fresh ginger
- 5 garlic cloves
- 1 teaspoon garam masala
- 1 teaspoon ground fennel
- 1 teaspoon ground cinnamon
- 1 teaspoon ground turmeric
- ½ to 1 teaspoon cayenne pepper
- ½ teaspoon ground cardamom
- 1 teaspoon kosher salt
- 1 pound (454 g) lamb sirloin chops

1. In a blender, combine the onion, ginger, garlic, garam masala, fennel, cinnamon, turmeric, cayenne, cardamom, and salt. Pulse until the onion is finely minced and the mixture forms a thick paste, 3 to 4 minutes. 2. Place the lamb chops in a large bowl. Slash the meat and fat with a sharp knife several times to allow the marinade to penetrate better. Add the spice paste to the bowl and toss the lamb to coat. Marinate at room temperature for 30 minutes or cover and refrigerate for up to 24 hours. 3. Place the lamb chops in a single layer in the air fryer basket. Set the air fryer to 325ºF (163ºC)

for 15 minutes, turning the chops halfway through the cooking time. Use a meat thermometer to ensure the lamb has reached an internal temperature of 145ºF (63ºC) (medium-rare).

Per Serving:

calories: 310 | fat: 20g | protein: 28g | carbs: 7g | net carbs: 6g | fiber: 1g

Spiced Beef Shami Kabob

Prep time: 15 minutes | Cook time: 35 minutes | Serves 4

- 1 pound (454 g) beef chunks, chopped
- 1 teaspoon ginger paste
- ½ teaspoon ground cumin
- 2 cups water
- ¼ cup almond flour
- 1 egg, beaten
- 1 tablespoon coconut oil

1. Put the beef chunks, ginger paste, ground cumin, and water in the Instant Pot. 2. Select Manual mode and set cooking time for 30 minutes on High Pressure. 3. When timer beeps, make a quick pressure release. Open the lid. 4. Drain the water from the meat. Transfer the beef in the blender. Add the almond flour and beaten egg. Blend until smooth. Shape the mixture into small meatballs. 5. Heat the coconut oil on Sauté mode and put the meatballs inside. 6. Cook for 2 minutes on each side or until golden brown. 7. Serve immediately.

Per Serving:

calories: 179 | fat: 10g | protein: 20g | carbs: 3g | net carbs: 3g | fiber: 0g

Roasted Garlic Beef

Prep time: 2 minutes | Cook time: 70 minutes | Serves 6

- 2 pounds (907 g) top round roast
- ½ cup beef broth
- 2 teaspoons salt
- 1 teaspoon black pepper
- 3 whole cloves garlic
- 1 bay leaf

1. Add the roast, broth, salt, pepper, garlic, and bay leaf to the pot. 2. Close the lid and seal the vent. Cook on High Pressure for 15 minutes. Let the steam naturally release for 15 minutes before Manually releasing. 3. Remove the beef from the pot and slice or shred it. Store it in an airtight container in the fridge or freezer.

Per Serving:

calories: 178 | fat: 4g | protein: 32g | carbs: 1g | net carbs: 1g | fiber: 0g

Easygoing Meatloaf

- 5 tablespoons no-sugar-added ketchup, divided
- 1½ pounds lean ground beef
- 2 large eggs
- ½ cup crushed pork rinds
- 1 small white onion, peeled and chopped
- 1 tablespoon Italian seasoning
- 1 teaspoon mustard powder
- 1 teaspoon soy sauce
- ½ teaspoon minced garlic
- ½ teaspoon black pepper

1. Preheat oven to 400°F. Grease a 9" × 5" × 2½" loaf pan. 2. In a large bowl, combine 3 tablespoons ketchup with all remaining ingredients until combined. 3. Add the mixture to the prepared pan. Top with remaining ketchup and cover with foil. 4. Bake 50–60 minutes. Serve warm.

Per Serving:

calories: 278 | fat: 14g | protein: 30g | carbs: 2g | net carbs: 2g | fiber: 0g

Hearty Beef and Red Cabbage Stew

- 2 tablespoons butter, at room temperature
- 1 onion, chopped
- 2 garlic cloves, minced
- 1½ pounds (680 g) beef stew meat, cubed
- 2½ cups beef stock
- 8 ounces (227 g) sugar-free tomato sauce
- 2 cups shredded red cabbage
- 1 tablespoon coconut aminos
- 2 bay leaves
- 1 teaspoon dried parsley flakes
- ½ teaspoon crushed red pepper flakes
- Sea salt and ground black pepper, to taste

1. Press the Sauté button to heat up the Instant Pot. Then, melt the butter. Cook the onion and garlic until softened. 2. Add beef stew meat and cook an additional 3 minutes or until browned. Stir the remaining ingredients into the Instant Pot. 3. Secure the lid. Choose Manual mode and High Pressure; cook for 15 minutes. Once cooking is complete, use a quick pressure release; carefully remove the lid. 4. Discard bay leaves and ladle into individual bowls. Enjoy!

Per Serving:

calories: 320 | fat: 16g | protein: 39g | carbs: 7g | net carbs: 5g | fiber: 2g

Savory Beef Meatball Stroganoff

- 1 pound (454 g) ground beef
- 1 egg
- 4 tablespoons heavy cream, divided
- 3 cloves garlic, minced
- 1 tablespoon chopped fresh parsley, plus more for garnish
- ½ teaspoon salt
- Pinch of black pepper
- 1 cup beef broth
- 8 ounces (227 g) sliced baby bella mushrooms
- ¼ cup sour cream
- 1 teaspoon xanthan gum

1. In a large bowl, combine the beef, egg, 2 tablespoons of the heavy cream, garlic, parsley, salt, and pepper. Use a spoon to work everything evenly into the beef. 2. Use a cookie scoop to divide out 24 meatballs, about 1 ounce (28 g) each. Roll them between your hands to round them out. 3. Add the broth and mushrooms to the pot. Place the meatballs on top of the mushrooms. 4. Close the lid and seal the vent. Cook on High Pressure for 12 minutes. Quick release the steam. Press Cancel. 5. Use a slotted spoon to transfer the meatballs from the pot to a bowl or platter. 6. Turn the pot to Sauté mode. Whisk in the sour cream and the remaining 2 tablespoons heavy cream. Once the broth begins to lightly boil, whisk in the xanthan gum. Continue whisking until a thin gravy consistency is reached, about 2 minutes. Pour the gravy on top of the meatballs. Garnish with fresh parsley.

Per Serving:

calories: 408 | fat: 27g | protein: 29g | carbs: 14g | net carbs: 6g | fiber: 8g

Fajita-Style Pork Shoulder

- 11 ounces (312 g) pork shoulder, boneless, sliced
- 1 teaspoon fajita seasoning
- 2 tablespoons butter
- ½ cup water

1. Sprinkle the meat with fajita seasoning and put in the instant pot. 2. Add butter and cook it on Sauté mode for 5 minutes. 3. Then stir the pork strips and add water. 4. Seal the instant pot lid and set the Manual mode (High Pressure). 5. Set timer for 40 minutes. 6. When the time is running out, make the natural pressure release for 10 minutes.

Per Serving:

calories: 375 | fat: 30g | protein: 24g | carbs: 1g | net carbs: 1g | fiber: 0g

Cuban-Style Pork Shoulder

Prep time: 20 minutes | Cook time: 35 minutes | Serves 3

- 9 ounces (255 g) pork shoulder, boneless, chopped
- 1 tablespoon avocado oil
- 1 teaspoon ground cumin
- ½ teaspoon ground black pepper
- ¼ cup apple cider vinegar
- 1 cup water

1. In the mixing bowl, mix up avocado oil, ground cumin, ground black pepper, and apple cider vinegar. 2. Mix up pork shoulder and spice mixture together and transfer on the foil. Wrap the meat mixture. 3. Pour water and insert the steamer rack in the instant pot. 4. Put the wrapped pork shoulder on the rack. Close and seal the lid. 5. Cook the Cuban pork for 35 minutes. 6. Then allow the natural pressure release for 10 minutes.

Per Serving:
calories: 262 | fat: 19g | protein: 20g | carbs: 1g | net carbs: 1g | fiber: 0g

Flavorful Pork Wraps

Prep time: 10 minutes | Cook time: 30 minutes | Serves 6

- 6 bacon slices
- 2 tablespoons fresh parsley, chopped
- 1 pound pork cutlets, sliced
- ⅓ cup ricotta cheese
- 1 tablespoon coconut oil
- ¼ cup onions, chopped
- 3 garlic cloves, peeled and minced
- 2 tablespoons Parmesan cheese, grated
- 15 ounces canned diced tomatoes
- ⅓ cup vegetable stock
- Salt and black pepper, to taste
- ½ teaspoon Italian seasoning

1. Use a meat pounder to flatten the pork pieces. Set the bacon slices on top of each piece, then divide the parsley, ricotta cheese, and Parmesan cheese. Roll each pork piece and secure with a toothpick. Set a pan over medium heat and warm oil, cook the pork rolls until browned, and remove to a plate. 2. Add in onions and garlic, and cook for 5 minutes. Place in the stock and cook for 3 minutes. Get rid of the toothpicks from the rolls and return to the pan. Stir in the pepper, salt, tomatoes, and Italian seasoning, bring to a boil, set heat to medium-low, and cook for 20 minutes covered. Split among bowls to serve.

Per Serving:
calories: 259 | fat: 15g | protein: 21g | carbs: 8g | net carbs: 6g | fiber: 2g

Herb-Infused Rosemary Pork Belly

Prep time: 10 minutes | Cook time: 75 minutes | Serves 4

- 10 ounces (283 g) pork belly
- 1 teaspoon dried rosemary
- ½ teaspoon dried thyme
- ¼ teaspoon ground cinnamon
- 1 teaspoon salt
- 1 cup water

1. Rub the pork belly with dried rosemary, thyme, ground cinnamon, and salt and transfer in the instant pot bowl. 2. Add water, close and seal the lid. 3. Cook the pork belly on Manual mode (High Pressure) for 75 minutes. 4. Remove the cooked pork belly from the instant pot and slice it into servings.

Per Serving:
calories: 329 | fat: 19g | protein: 33g | carbs: 0g | net carbs: 0g | fiber: 0g

Hearty Ground Beef Cabbage Bake

Prep time: 5 minutes | Cook time: 4 minutes | Serves 4

- 1 pound (454 g) 85% lean ground beef
- 2 cups shredded white cabbage
- 1 cup salsa
- 1 teaspoon salt
- 1 tablespoon chili powder
- ½ teaspoon cumin
- ½ cup water
- 1 cup shredded Cheddar cheese

1. Press the Sauté button and brown ground beef. Once fully cooked, add remaining ingredients except for cheese. 2. Click lid closed. Press the Manual button and adjust timer for 4 minutes. When timer beeps, quick-release the pressure and stir in Cheddar.

Per Serving:
calories: 393 | fat: 23g | protein: 30g | carbs: 5g | net carbs: 3g | fiber: 2g

Juicy Pork Meatballs

- 1 pound (454 g) ground pork
- 1 large egg, whisked
- ½ teaspoon garlic powder
- ½ teaspoon salt
- ½ teaspoon ground ginger
- ¼ teaspoon crushed red pepper flakes
- 1 medium scallion, trimmed and sliced

1. Combine all ingredients in a large bowl. Spoon out 2 tablespoons mixture and roll into a ball. Repeat to form eighteen meatballs total.
2. Place meatballs into ungreased air fryer basket. Adjust the temperature to 400°F (204°C) and air fry for 12 minutes, shaking the basket three times throughout cooking. Meatballs will be browned and have an internal temperature of at least 145°F (63°C) when done. Serve warm.

Per Serving:

calories: 77 | fat: 5g | protein: 7g | carbs: 0g | net carbs: 0g | fiber: 0g

Pork Tenderloin with Creamy Avocado Lime Sauce

Marinade:

- ½ cup lime juice
- Grated zest of 1 lime
- 2 teaspoons stevia glycerite, or ¼ teaspoon liquid stevia
- 3 cloves garlic, minced

Avocado Lime Sauce:

- 1 medium-sized ripe avocado, roughly chopped
- ½ cup full-fat sour cream (or coconut cream for dairy-free)
- Grated zest of 1 lime
- Juice of 1 lime
- 2 cloves garlic, roughly chopped

- 1½ teaspoons fine sea salt
- 1 teaspoon chili powder, or more for more heat
- 1 teaspoon smoked paprika
- 1 pound (454 g) pork tenderloin

- ½ teaspoon fine sea salt
- ¼ teaspoon ground black pepper
- Chopped fresh cilantro leaves, for garnish
- Lime slices, for serving
- Pico de gallo, for serving

1. In a medium-sized casserole dish, stir together all the marinade ingredients until well combined. Add the tenderloin and coat it well in the marinade. Cover and place in the fridge to marinate for 2 hours or overnight. 2. Spray the air fryer basket with avocado oil. Preheat the air fryer to 400°F (204°C). 3. Remove the pork from the marinade and place it in the air fryer basket. Air fry for 13 to 15 minutes, until the internal temperature of the pork is 145°F (63°C), flipping after 7 minutes. Remove the pork from the air fryer and place it on a cutting board. Allow it to rest for 8 to 10 minutes, then cut it into ½-inch-thick slices. 4. While the pork cooks, make the avocado lime sauce: Place all the sauce ingredients in a food processor and purée until smooth. Taste and adjust the seasoning to your liking. 5. Place the pork slices on a serving platter and spoon the avocado lime sauce on top. Garnish with cilantro leaves and serve with lime slices and pico de gallo. 6. Store leftovers in an airtight container in the fridge for up to 4 days. Reheat in a preheated 400°F (204°C) air fryer for 5 minutes, or until heated through.

Per Serving:

calories: 324 | fat: 18g | protein: 25g | carbs: 15g | net carbs: 7g | fiber: 8g

Chapter **5**

Fish and Seafood

Chilean Sea Bass with Olive Relish

Prep time: 10 minutes | Cook time: 10 minutes | Serves 2

- Olive oil spray
- 2 (6-ounce / 170-g) Chilean sea bass fillets or other firm-fleshed white fish
- 3 tablespoons extra-virgin olive oil
- ½ teaspoon ground cumin
- ½ teaspoon kosher salt
- ½ teaspoon black pepper
- ⅓ cup pitted green olives, diced
- ¼ cup finely diced onion
- 1 teaspoon chopped capers

1. Start by spraying the air fryer basket with olive oil spray to prevent sticking. Drizzle the fish fillets with olive oil, then sprinkle them with cumin, salt, and pepper to season. Place the seasoned fish fillets in the air fryer basket in a single layer. Set the air fryer to 325°F (163°C) and cook for 10 minutes, or until the fish flakes easily with a fork. 2. While the fish is cooking, prepare the relish by combining the olives, onion, and capers in a small bowl. Stir the ingredients together until well mixed. 3.

Per Serving:

calories: 379 | fat: 26g | protein: 32g | carbs: 3g | net carbs: 2g | fiber: 1g

Rainbow Salmon Kebabs

Prep time: 10 minutes | Cook time: 8 minutes | Serves 2

- 6 ounces (170 g) boneless, skinless salmon, cut into 1-inch cubes
- ¼ medium red onion, peeled and cut into 1-inch pieces
- ½ medium yellow bell pepper, seeded and cut into 1-inch pieces
- ½ medium zucchini, trimmed and cut into ½-inch slices
- 1 tablespoon olive oil
- ½ teaspoon salt
- ¼ teaspoon ground black pepper

1. Begin by preparing your skewers. Using a 6-inch skewer, thread on one piece of salmon, followed by one piece of onion, one piece of bell pepper, and one piece of zucchini. Repeat this pattern until you have made a total of four kebabs. Once assembled, drizzle the kebabs with olive oil and sprinkle them with salt and black pepper to season. 2. Place the kebabs in the ungreased air fryer basket, ensuring they are arranged in a single layer for even cooking. Adjust the air fryer temperature to 400°F (204°C) and set the timer for 8 minutes. Be sure to turn the kebabs halfway through the cooking time for even browning. 3. The salmon is done when it easily flakes and reaches an internal temperature of at least 145°F (63°C), while the vegetables should be tender. Once cooked, remove the kebabs from the air fryer and serve warm. Enjoy your delicious salmon and vegetable kebabs!

Per Serving:

calories: 270 | fat: 16g | protein: 25g | carbs: 9g | net carbs: 6g | fiber: 3g

Classic Fish Sticks with Tartar Sauce

Prep time: 10 minutes | Cook time: 12 to 15 minutes | Serves 4

- 1½ pounds (680 g) cod fillets, cut into 1-inch strips
- 1 teaspoon salt
- ½ teaspoon freshly ground black pepper

Tartar Sauce:

- ½ cup sour cream
- ½ cup mayonnaise
- 3 tablespoons chopped dill pickle
- 2 eggs
- ¾ cup almond flour
- ¼ cup grated Parmesan cheese

- 2 tablespoons capers, drained and chopped
- ½ teaspoon dried dill
- 1 tablespoon dill pickle liquid (optional)

1. Preheat your air fryer to 400°F (204°C). 2. Season the cod fillets with salt and black pepper, then set them aside to allow the seasoning to penetrate. 3. In a shallow bowl, lightly beat the eggs. In a second shallow bowl, combine the almond flour and Parmesan cheese, stirring until thoroughly mixed. 4. Working with a few pieces of cod at a time, dip each piece into the egg mixture, allowing any excess to drip off, and then coat it in the almond flour and Parmesan mixture. Press lightly to ensure an even coating. 5. Arrange the coated fish in a single layer in the air fryer basket. If needed, work in batches. Lightly spray the fish with olive oil. Air fry for 12 to 15 minutes, pausing halfway through to turn the fish for even cooking. The fish is done when it flakes easily with a fork. Let the fish sit in the basket for a few minutes before serving. 6. To make the tartar sauce, combine sour cream, mayonnaise, chopped pickles, capers, and dill in a small bowl. If you prefer a thinner consistency, stir in a little pickle liquid. Serve the crispy cod with the tartar sauce on the side. Enjoy!

Per Serving:

calories: 382 | fat: 23g | protein: 36g | carbs: 7g | net carbs: 5g | fiber: 2g

Stuffed Trout

- 2 (7-ounce/200-g) head-off, gutted trout
- 2 tablespoons refined avocado oil or melted coconut oil
- 2 teaspoons dried dill weed
- 1 teaspoon dried thyme leaves
- ½ teaspoon ground black pepper
- ¼ teaspoon finely ground gray sea salt
- ½ lemon, sliced
- 1 green onion, green part only, sliced in half lengthwise

1. Preheat your oven to 400°F (205°C). 2. Place the fish in a large cast-iron frying pan or on an unlined rimmed baking sheet. Drizzle the fish with oil, ensuring it is well coated. In a small bowl, combine the dried herbs, pepper, and salt. Sprinkle this herb mixture generously over the fish, covering the top, bottom, and inside. 3. Carefully open the fish and insert slices of lemon and green onion inside the cavity. Lay the fish flat on the pan or baking sheet, then transfer it to the preheated oven. Bake for up to 20 minutes, or until the fish reaches your desired level of doneness. 4. Once cooked, remove the fish from the oven and cut it in half before transferring it to a serving platter. Enjoy your delicious baked fish!

Per Serving:
calories: 219 | fat: 12g | protein: 27g | carbs: 1g | net carbs: 1g | fiber: 0g

Spicy Grilled Shrimp with Mojo Verde

- ½ cup lime or lemon juice
- 3 teaspoons minced garlic
- ¼ red onion, thinly sliced
- 12 jumbo shrimp (peels on), Dipping Sauce:
- 3 loosely packed cups fresh cilantro leaves
- ½ cup MCT oil or extra-virgin olive oil
- deveined and butterflied
- 2 teaspoons cayenne pepper
- 1 teaspoon ground cumin
- 1 teaspoon fine sea salt
- 2 tablespoons minced garlic
- 2 teaspoons coconut vinegar
- 1 teaspoon fine sea salt
- ½ teaspoon ground cumin

1. Begin by preheating your grill to medium-high heat. While the grill is heating up, soak 4 wooden skewers in water to prevent them from burning during grilling. 2. In a shallow baking dish, pour in the lime juice and add minced garlic and chopped onion. Toss in the shrimp and let them marinate for about 15 minutes. This will infuse the shrimp with flavor while you prepare the spices and dipping sauce. 3. In a small bowl, combine cayenne pepper, cumin, and salt. Mix well to create a spice blend that will enhance the shrimp's flavor. Set this aside for later use. 4. For the dipping sauce, gather all the ingredients and place them in a food processor or blender. Pulse until the mixture is smooth and well combined. Taste the sauce and adjust the seasoning by adding more salt if necessary. 5. After the shrimp have marinated, remove them from the dish and generously sprinkle the spice mixture over them, ensuring they are well coated. Thread 3 shrimp onto each skewer, making sure they are evenly spaced. Place the skewers on the grill and cook for 3 to 4 minutes on each side, or until the shrimp turn pink and are fully cooked. Once done, take them off the grill and serve each skewer with about ¼ cup of the prepared dipping sauce. 6. This dish is best enjoyed fresh off the grill, but if you have leftovers, you can store them in an airtight container in the refrigerator for up to 3 days. The shrimp can also be served cold. To reheat, simply place the shrimp in a skillet over medium heat and sauté until warmed through. Enjoy your delicious grilled shrimp skewers!

Per Serving:
calories: 365 | fat: 29g | protein: 21g | carbs: 5g | net carbs: 4g | fiber: 1g

Oregano Tilapia Fingers

- 1 pound (454 g) tilapia fillet
- ½ cup coconut flour
- 2 eggs, beaten
- ½ teaspoon ground paprika
- 1 teaspoon dried oregano
- 1 teaspoon avocado oil

1. Start by cutting the tilapia fillets into finger-sized strips. Sprinkle the cut fish fingers with ground paprika and dried oregano, ensuring they are evenly coated. 2. In a shallow bowl, beat a couple of eggs. Dip each tilapia finger into the beaten eggs, allowing any excess to drip off, and then coat them in coconut flour, pressing lightly to ensure the flour adheres well. 3. Preheat your air fryer to 370°F (188°C). Once preheated, place the coated tilapia fingers in the air fryer basket in a single layer. Lightly spray or drizzle the fish fingers with avocado oil for added crispiness. Cook for 9 minutes, or until the fish is golden brown and cooked through. 4. Carefully remove the tilapia fingers from the air fryer and serve immediately. Enjoy your crispy tilapia fingers!

Per Serving:
calories: 230 | fat: 8g | protein: 32g | carbs: 10g | net carbs: 7g | fiber: 3g

Garam Masala Fish

- 2 tablespoons sesame oil
- ½ teaspoon cumin seeds
- ½ cup chopped leeks
- 1 teaspoon ginger-garlic paste
- 1 pound (454 g) cod fillets, boneless and sliced
- 2 ripe tomatoes, chopped
- 1½ tablespoons fresh lemon juice
- ½ teaspoon garam masala
- ½ teaspoon turmeric powder
- 1 tablespoon chopped fresh dill leaves
- 1 tablespoon chopped fresh curry leaves
- 1 tablespoon chopped fresh parsley leaves
- Coarse sea salt, to taste
- ½ teaspoon smoked cayenne pepper
- ¼ teaspoon ground black pepper, or more to taste

1. Set the Instant Pot to the Sauté function. Add the sesame oil and heat it until hot. Once hot, sauté the cumin seeds for about 30 seconds, allowing them to become fragrant. 2. Add the leeks to the pot and cook for another 2 minutes, stirring occasionally, until they become translucent. Then, add the ginger-garlic paste and cook for an additional 40 seconds, stirring to combine. 3. Stir in the remaining ingredients, mixing well to ensure everything is evenly combined. 4. Lock the lid of the Instant Pot in place. Select the Manual mode and set the cooking time for 6 minutes at Low Pressure. 5. When the timer beeps, perform a quick pressure release by carefully turning the valve to release the steam. Once the pressure has fully released, carefully remove the lid. 6. Serve the dish immediately, enjoying the rich flavors and aromas.

Per Serving:

calories: 166 | fat: 8g | protein: 18g | carbs: 6g | net carbs: 4g | fiber: 2g

Lemon Butter Mahi Mahi

- 1 pound (454 g) mahi-mahi fillet
- 1 teaspoon grated lemon zest
- 1 tablespoon lemon juice
- 1 tablespoon butter, softened
- ½ teaspoon salt
- 1 cup water, for cooking

1. Cut the fish into 4 equal servings and sprinkle each piece with lemon zest, lemon juice, and salt. Rub softened butter over the fish to enhance flavor and moisture. 2. Place the seasoned fish in a baking pan in a single layer to ensure even cooking. 3. Pour water into the Instant Pot and insert the steamer rack. 4. Carefully place the baking pan with the fish on the steamer rack inside the Instant Pot. Close and seal the lid securely. 5. Set the Instant Pot to Manual mode and select High Pressure. Set the cooking time for 9 minutes. Once the cooking time is complete, perform a quick pressure release by carefully turning the valve to release the steam. 6. Once the pressure has fully released, carefully open the lid and check the fish for doneness. Serve immediately and enjoy your delicious Mahi Mahi!

Per Serving:

calories: 128 | fat: 4g | protein: 21g | carbs: 0g | net carbs: 0g | fiber: 0g

Fish and Scallop Ceviche

- 4 ounces (113 g) shrimp, peeled and chopped
- 1 (4-ounce / 113-g) white fish fillet, chopped into bite-size pieces
- 4 ounces (113 g) bay or other small scallops
- ¼ small red onion, chopped
- ½ jalapeño pepper, seeded and finely chopped
- 1 garlic clove, minced
- ½ teaspoon pink Himalayan sea salt
- ¼ teaspoon freshly ground
- black pepper
- 3 or 4 limes
- ½ medium cucumber, peeled and chopped
- ½ avocado, slightly firm, chopped
- ⅓ cup grape tomatoes, halved
- 3 tablespoons chopped fresh cilantro
- 2 teaspoons extra-virgin olive oil
- Firm lettuce leaves, for wraps

1. Set the Instant Pot to the Sauté function. Add the sesame oil and heat it until hot. Once hot, sauté the cumin seeds for about 30 seconds, allowing them to become fragrant. 2. Add the leeks to the pot and cook for another 2 minutes, stirring occasionally, until they become translucent. Then, add the ginger-garlic paste and cook for an additional 40 seconds, stirring to combine. 3. Stir in the remaining ingredients, mixing well to ensure everything is evenly combined. 4. Lock the lid of the Instant Pot in place. Select the Manual mode and set the cooking time for 6 minutes at Low Pressure. 5. When the timer beeps, perform a quick pressure release by carefully turning the valve to release the steam. Once the pressure has fully released, carefully remove the lid. 6. Serve the dish immediately, enjoying the rich flavors and aromas.

Per Serving:

calories: 211 | fat: 9g | protein: 21g | carbs: 13g | net carbs: 9g | fiber: 4g

Sheet Pan Garlic Butter Shrimp

Prep time: 10 minutes | Cook time: 10 minutes | serves 4

- 1½ pounds medium shrimp, peeled and deveined
- ½ cup (1 stick) salted butter, melted
- ¼ cup chopped fresh flat-leaf parsley
- 2 cloves garlic, minced
- Pinch of salt
- Pinch of ground black pepper
- 1 lemon, sliced

1. Preheat your oven to 400°F (200°C) and line a sheet pan with parchment paper. 2. Pat the shrimp dry and arrange them in a single layer on the lined pan. 3. In a small bowl, mix together the melted butter, chopped parsley, minced garlic, salt, and pepper. Pour the butter mixture evenly over the shrimp, ensuring they are well coated. 4. Place lemon slices on top of the shrimp for added flavor. Bake in the preheated oven for 8 to 10 minutes, or until the shrimp are pink and opaque. 5. Serve immediately and enjoy your delicious shrimp dish!

Per Serving:

calories: 320 | fat: 24g | protein: 25g | carbs: 1g | net carbs: 1g | fiber: 0g

Spicy Shrimp Fried Rice

Prep time: 15 minutes | Cook time: 15 minutes | Serves 4

- ¼ teaspoon cayenne pepper
- ¼ teaspoon chili powder
- ¼ teaspoon paprika
- ¼ teaspoon pink Himalayan salt
- ¼ teaspoon ground black pepper
- 1 pound medium-sized shrimp, peeled and deveined
- 2 tablespoons ghee, divided
- 4 cups riced cauliflower (see Tip)
- ½ medium-sized white onion, finely chopped
- 2 teaspoons minced fresh ginger
- 1 cup fresh broccoli florets, chopped
- 3 tablespoons soy sauce
- 1 tablespoon Sriracha sauce
- 1½ teaspoons unseasoned rice wine vinegar
- 2 large eggs
- 2 teaspoons toasted sesame oil

For Garnish (Optional):

- Sliced scallions
- Black and white sesame seeds

1. In a medium-sized bowl, combine the cayenne, chili powder, paprika, salt, and pepper. Mix well to blend the spices, then add the shrimp and toss until they are evenly coated in the seasoning blend. 2. Heat 1 tablespoon of ghee in a large skillet over medium-

high heat. Once hot, add the seasoned shrimp and cook for about 2 minutes on each side, or until they turn pink. Remove the shrimp from the skillet and transfer them to a small bowl; set aside. 3. In the same skillet, add the remaining tablespoon of ghee and pour in the riced cauliflower. Spread it out with a spatula so it lies flat on the skillet surface. Cook for 3 to 5 minutes, allowing it to crisp up. 4. Stir the riced cauliflower, then add the onion and ginger. Cook for 2 minutes, or until the onion is slightly tender. Add the broccoli and cook for an additional 1 to 2 minutes, until it turns bright green. Pour in the soy sauce, Sriracha, and vinegar, and combine everything using the spatula. 5. Create a well in the center of the skillet and crack in the eggs. Scramble the eggs with the spatula, then mix them into the rest of the contents in the skillet. 6. Add the cooked shrimp back into the skillet and toss everything together to combine. Drizzle with sesame oil and garnish with sliced scallions and sesame seeds, if desired. Serve immediately. 7. For leftovers, store them in a sealed container in the refrigerator for up to 4 days. Reheat in the microwave for 60 to 90 seconds before serving. Enjoy your flavorful shrimp and cauliflower rice dish!

Per Serving:

calories: 283 | fat: 13g | protein: 32g | carbs: 13g | net carbs: 9g | fiber: 4g

Tuna Salad with Tomatoes and Peppers

Prep time: 10 minutes | Cook time: 4 minutes | Serves 4

- 1½ cups water
- 1 pound (454 g) tuna steaks
- 1 green bell pepper, sliced
- 1 red bell pepper, sliced
- 2 Roma tomatoes, sliced
- 1 head lettuce
- 1 red onion, chopped
- 2 tablespoons Kalamata olives, pitted and halved
- 2 tablespoons extra-virgin olive oil
- 2 tablespoons balsamic vinegar
- ½ teaspoon chili flakes
- Sea salt, to taste

1. Add the water to the Instant Pot and insert a steamer basket. 2. Arrange the tuna steaks in the basket. Put the bell peppers and tomato slices on top. 3. Lock the lid. Select the Manual mode and set the cooking time for 4 minutes at High Pressure. 4. When the timer beeps, perform a quick pressure release. Carefully remove the lid. 5. Flake the fish with a fork. 6. Divide the lettuce leaves among 4 serving plates to make a bed for your salad. Add the onion and olives. Drizzle with the olive oil and balsamic vinegar. 7. Season with the chili flakes and salt. Place the prepared fish, tomatoes, and bell peppers on top. 8. Serve immediately.

Per Serving:

calories: 170 | fat: 5g | protein: 24g | carbs: 8g | net carbs: 6g | fiber: 2g

Baked Tilapia and Parmesan

Prep time: 10 minutes | Cook time: 15 minutes | Serves 4

- 4 tablespoons (½ stick) butter, melted
- 2 teaspoons garlic salt
- 1 teaspoon freshly ground black pepper
- 4 (4-ounce / 113-g) tilapia fillets, patted dry
- 4 ounces (113 g) grated Parmesan cheese
- 4 ounces (113 g) crushed pork rinds

1. Preheat your oven to 400°F (205°C). While the oven is heating, line a baking sheet with parchment paper and set it aside. 2. In a small bowl, combine the melted butter, garlic salt, and pepper, mixing well. Place the tilapia fillets on the prepared baking sheet, then drizzle or brush the butter mixture evenly over each fillet. 3. Next, sprinkle each fillet with Parmesan cheese and crushed pork rinds, ensuring they are evenly coated for a crispy topping. 4. Bake the tilapia in the preheated oven for about 13 minutes, or until the fish is cooked through and flakes easily with a fork. After 13 minutes, turn the oven up to broil and broil the fillets for an additional 2 minutes, or until the topping is golden and crispy. 5. Once done, remove the baking sheet from the oven and let the tilapia cool slightly before serving. Enjoy your deliciously baked tilapia!

Per Serving:
1 fillet: calories: 372 | fat: 24g | protein: 38g | carbs: 1g | net carbs: 1g | fiber: 0g

Louisiana Shrimp Gumbo

Prep time: 10 minutes | Cook time: 4 minutes | Serves 6

- 1 pound (454 g) shrimp
- ¼ cup chopped celery stalk
- 1 chili pepper, chopped
- ¼ cup chopped okra
- 1 tablespoon coconut oil
- 2 cups chicken broth
- 1 teaspoon sugar-free tomato paste

1. Begin by adding all the ingredients to the Instant Pot. Stir the mixture until you achieve a light red color, ensuring that everything is well combined. 2. Once mixed, close and seal the lid of the Instant Pot securely. 3. Set the Instant Pot to Manual mode and select High Pressure. Cook the meal for 4 minutes. 4. After the cooking time is complete, allow for a natural pressure release for 10 minutes. This means you should not touch the pressure release valve during this time. After 10 minutes, you can carefully release any remaining pressure by turning the valve to the venting position. Once the pressure has fully released, open the lid and serve your meal. Enjoy!

Per Serving:
calories: 126 | fat: 4g | protein: 19g | carbs: 2g | net carbs: 2g | fiber: 0g

Lime Lobster Tails

Prep time: 10 minutes | Cook time: 6 minutes | Serves 4

- 4 lobster tails, peeled
- 2 tablespoons lime juice
- ½ teaspoon dried basil
- ½ teaspoon coconut oil, melted

1. In a mixing bowl, combine the lobster tails with lime juice, dried basil, and melted coconut oil. Toss the lobster tails until they are evenly coated with the mixture. 2. Preheat your air fryer to 380°F (193°C). Once preheated, place the lobster tails in the air fryer basket in a single layer. Cook for 6 minutes, or until the lobster is cooked through and opaque. 3. Carefully remove the lobster tails from the air fryer and serve immediately. Enjoy your delicious air-fried lobster tails!

Per Serving:
calories: 110 | fat: 2g | protein: 22g | carbs: 1g | net carbs: 1g | fiber: 0g

Prosciutto-Wrapped Haddock

Prep time: 10 minutes | Cook time: 15 minutes | Serves 4

- 4 (4 ounces) haddock fillets, about 1 inch thick
- Sea salt, for seasoning
- Freshly ground black pepper, for seasoning
- 4 slices prosciutto (2 ounces)
- 3 tablespoons garlic-infused olive oil
- Juice and zest of 1 lemon

1. Preheat your oven to 350°F (175°C) and line a baking sheet with parchment paper. 2. Prepare the fish by patting it dry with paper towels, then season it lightly on both sides with salt and pepper. Carefully wrap the prosciutto around the fish, ensuring it is tightly secured without tearing. 3. Place the wrapped fish on the prepared baking sheet and drizzle it with olive oil. Bake in the preheated oven for 15 to 17 minutes, or until the fish flakes easily with a fork. 4. To serve, divide the fish among four plates and top with lemon zest and a drizzle of fresh lemon juice. Enjoy your delicious dish!

Per Serving:
calories: 282 | fat: 18g | protein: 29g | carbs: 1g | net carbs: 1g | fiber: 0g

Baked Monkfish

- 2 teaspoons olive oil
- 1 cup celery, sliced
- 2 bell peppers, sliced
- 1 teaspoon dried thyme
- ½ teaspoon dried marjoram
- ½ teaspoon dried rosemary
- 2 monkfish fillets
- 1 tablespoon coconut aminos
- 2 tablespoons lime juice
- Coarse salt and ground black pepper, to taste
- 1 teaspoon cayenne pepper
- ½ cup Kalamata olives, pitted and sliced

1. Begin by heating olive oil in a nonstick skillet over medium heat for about 1 minute. Once the oil is hot, add the chopped celery and bell peppers. Sauté the vegetables until they become tender, which should take around 4 minutes. Once cooked, sprinkle the mixture with thyme, marjoram, and rosemary, then set it aside. 2. In a mixing bowl, toss the fish fillets with coconut aminos, lime juice, salt, black pepper, and cayenne pepper until they are well coated. 3. Lightly grease the air fryer basket and place the seasoned fish fillets inside. Set the air fryer to 390°F (199°C) and cook the fish for 8 minutes. 4. After 8 minutes, carefully turn the fillets over, add the olives

Per Serving:

calories: 278 | fat: 8g | protein: 34g | carbs: 16g | net carbs: 12g | fiber: 4g

Trout and Fennel Parcels

- ½ pound deboned trout, butterflied
- Salt and black pepper to season
- 3 tablespoons olive oil + extra for tossing
- 4 sprigs rosemary
- 4 sprigs thyme
- 4 butter cubes
- 1 cup thinly sliced fennel
- 1 medium red onion, sliced
- 8 lemon slices
- 3 teaspoons capers to garnish

1. Preheat your oven to 400ºF (200ºC). While the oven is heating, cut out pieces of parchment paper large enough to create individual packets for each trout. 2. In a mixing bowl, combine the sliced fennel and onion with a drizzle of olive oil, tossing to coat. Divide this mixture and place it in the center of each piece of parchment paper. 3. Lay a trout on top of each mound of vegetables. Drizzle a little more olive oil over the fish, then season with a pinch of salt and black pepper. Add a sprig of rosemary and thyme to each fish, along with a cube of butter. Finally, place a few lemon slices on top of each trout. 4. Carefully fold the parchment paper over the fish and vegetables to create a sealed packet, ensuring it is tightly closed to trap in the steam. Arrange the packets on a baking sheet. 5. Bake in the preheated oven for 15 minutes. Once done, remove the packets from the oven and let them cool slightly before opening. 6. To serve, plate the trout and garnish with capers. Pair the fish with a delicious squash mash for a complete meal. Enjoy your flavorful dish!

Per Serving:

calories: 313 | fat: 22g | protein: 22g | carbs: 10g | net carbs: 8g | fiber: 2g

Greek Shrimp with Tomatoes and Feta

- 3 tablespoons unsalted butter
- 1 tablespoon garlic
- ½ teaspoon red pepper flakes, or more as needed
- 1½ cups chopped onion
- 1 (14½-ounce / 411-g) can diced tomatoes, undrained
- 1 teaspoon dried oregano
- 1 teaspoon salt
- 1 pound (454 g) frozen shrimp, peeled
- 1 cup crumbled feta cheese
- ½ cup sliced black olives
- ¼ cup chopped parsley

1. Begin by pouring water into the Instant Pot and placing a steamer basket inside. 2. Arrange the tuna steaks in the steamer basket, then layer the bell peppers and tomato slices on top of the fish. 3. Secure the lid on the Instant Pot. Select the Manual mode and set the cooking time to 4 minutes at High Pressure. 4. Once the timer goes off, carefully perform a quick pressure release to release the steam. Gently remove the lid once the pressure has fully released. 5. Use a fork to flake the cooked tuna steaks into bite-sized pieces. 6. On four serving plates, divide the lettuce leaves to create a fresh bed for your salad. Top the lettuce with sliced onion and olives. Drizzle the salad with olive oil and balsamic vinegar for added flavor. 7. Season the salad with chili flakes and salt to taste. Finally, place the flaked tuna, along with the cooked tomatoes and bell peppers, on top of the salad. 8. Serve the salad immediately while it's fresh and warm. Enjoy your delicious and healthy meal!

Per Serving:

calories: 361 | fat: 22g | protein: 30g | carbs: 13g | net carbs: 11g | fiber: 2g

Curried Fish Stew

Prep time: 10 minutes | Cook time: 20 minutes | Serves 6

- 1 tablespoon olive oil
- 1 medium onion, chopped
- 3 garlic cloves, minced
- 1 tablespoon tomato paste
- 2 tablespoons curry powder
- 1 head cauliflower, chopped
- 2 cups fish broth, or vegetable broth
- 1½ pounds (680 g) firm
- whitefish (cod or halibut), cubed
- 1 teaspoon ground cayenne pepper (more or less depending on your taste)
- Salt, to taste
- Freshly ground black pepper, to taste
- 1 (13½-ounce / 383-g) can full-fat coconut milk

1. In a large saucepan over medium heat, add the olive oil and allow it to heat up. 2. Once the oil is hot, add the chopped onion and minced garlic. Sauté for 5 to 7 minutes, stirring occasionally, until the onion is softened and translucent. 3. Stir in the tomato paste, curry powder, and cauliflower florets. Cook for an additional 1 to 2 minutes, allowing the flavors to meld. 4. While stirring, slowly pour in the broth, bringing the mixture to a simmer. Once simmering, add the fish to the pot. Cook for 10 to 15 minutes, or until the fish is opaque and cooked through. Season the dish with cayenne pepper, salt, and freshly ground black pepper to taste. 5. Finally, stir in the coconut milk and let it simmer on low heat until ready to serve. If

Per Serving:

calories: 373 | fat: 21g | protein: 33g | carbs: 13g | net carbs: 8g | fiber: 5g

Foil-Pack Haddock with Spinach

Prep time: 15 minutes | Cook time: 15 minutes | Serves 4

- 12 ounces (340 g) haddock fillet
- 1 cup spinach
- 1 tablespoon avocado oil
- 1 teaspoon minced garlic
- ½ teaspoon ground coriander
- 1 cup water, for cooking

1. Begin by blending the spinach until smooth, then mix it with avocado oil, ground coriander, and minced garlic to create a flavorful mixture. 2. Next, cut the haddock into 4 fillets and place them on a piece of foil. 3. Spread the spinach mixture evenly over the fish fillets. 4. Pour water into the Instant Pot and insert the rack. Place the foil with the haddock on the rack. 5. Close and seal the lid of the Instant Pot, then set it to Manual (High Pressure) and cook the haddock for 15 minutes. 6. Once the cooking time is complete,

perform a quick pressure release to release the steam. Enjoy your delicious haddock with spinach!

Per Serving:

calories: 103 | fat: 1g | protein: 21g | carbs: 1g | net carbs: 1g | fiber: 0g

Almond Catfish

Prep time: 10 minutes | Cook time: 12 minutes | Serves 4

- 2 pounds (907 g) catfish fillet
- ½ cup almond flour
- 2 eggs, beaten
- 1 teaspoon salt
- 1 teaspoon avocado oil

1. Start by sprinkling the catfish fillet with salt to season it. Then, dip the seasoned fillet into the beaten eggs, ensuring it is fully coated. 2. Next, coat the fish in almond flour, pressing gently to ensure an even layer adheres to the fillet. Place the coated fish in the air fryer basket. Lightly spray or sprinkle the fish with avocado oil to help it crisp up during cooking. 3. Set the air fryer to cook the fish at 380°F (193°C) for 6 minutes on one side. After 6 minutes, carefully flip the fish and cook for an additional 6 minutes on the other side, or until the fish is golden brown and cooked through. 4. Once done, remove the catfish from the air fryer and serve immediately. Enjoy your crispy, delicious catfish!

Per Serving:

calories: 360 | fat: 21g | protein: 36g | carbs: 7g | net carbs: 5g | fiber: 2g

Chili Tilapia

Prep time: 5 minutes | Cook time: 20 minutes | Serves 4

- 4 tilapia fillets, boneless
- 1 teaspoon chili flakes
- 1 teaspoon dried oregano
- 1 tablespoon avocado oil
- 1 teaspoon mustard

1. Begin by seasoning the tilapia fillets with chili flakes, dried oregano, avocado oil, and mustard, ensuring they are well coated before placing them in the air fryer. 2. Cook the fillets for 10 minutes on each side at a temperature of 360°F (182°C).

Per Serving:

calories: 155 | fat: 7g | protein: 23g | carbs: 1g | net carbs: 1g | fiber: 0g

Chunky Fish Soup with Tomatoes

- 2 teaspoons olive oil
- 1 yellow onion, chopped
- 1 bell pepper, sliced
- 1 celery, diced
- 2 garlic cloves, minced
- 3 cups fish stock
- 2 ripe tomatoes, crushed
- ¾ pound (340 g) haddock fillets
- 1 cup shrimp
- 1 tablespoon sweet Hungarian paprika
- 1 teaspoon hot Hungarian paprika
- ½ teaspoon caraway seeds

1. Begin by setting the Instant Pot to the Sauté function. Pour in the oil and allow it to heat up. Once the oil is hot, toss in the onions and sauté them until they become tender and aromatic. 2. Next, incorporate the bell pepper, celery, and garlic, continuing to sauté until all the vegetables are softened. 3. Then, mix in the remaining ingredients thoroughly. 4. Secure the lid in place. Choose the Manual mode and adjust the cooking time to 5 minutes at High Pressure. 5. When the timer signals that cooking is complete, execute a quick pressure release. Carefully lift the lid away. 6. Finally, ladle the mixture into serving bowls and enjoy it while it's hot.

Per Serving:
calories: 177 | fat: 5g | protein: 26g | carbs: 8g | net carbs: 6g | fiber: 2g

Coconut Curry Mussels

- 3 pounds mussels, cleaned, de-bearded
- 1 cup minced shallots
- 3 tablespoons minced garlic
- 1½ cups coconut milk
- 2 cups dry white wine
- 2 teaspoons red curry powder
- ⅓ cup coconut oil
- ⅓ cup chopped green onions
- ⅓ cup chopped parsley

1. Begin by pouring the wine into a spacious saucepan and gently cooking the shallots and garlic over low heat. Afterward, incorporate the coconut milk and red curry powder, allowing it to simmer for 3 minutes. 2. Next, add the mussels and steam them for 7 minutes, or until their shells have opened. Using a slotted spoon, transfer the mussels to a bowl while leaving the sauce in the pan. Discard any mussels that remain closed at this stage. 3. Mix the coconut oil into the sauce, turn off the heat, and then fold in the parsley and green onions. Serve the sauce right away alongside a butternut squash mash.

Per Serving:
calories: 275 | fat: 19g | protein: 23g | carbs: 3g | net carbs: 2g | fiber: 1g

White Fish with Cauliflower

- ½ pound (227 g) cauliflower florets
- ½ teaspoon English mustard
- 2 tablespoons butter, room temperature
- ½ tablespoon cilantro,
- minced
- 2 tablespoons sour cream
- 2½ cups cooked white fish
- Salt and freshly cracked black pepper, to taste

1. Start by boiling the cauliflower until it is tender. Once cooked, purée the cauliflower in your blender until smooth, then transfer it to a mixing bowl. 2. Next, stir in the fish, cilantro, salt, and black pepper until well combined. 3. Add the sour cream, English mustard, and butter to the mixture, and mix thoroughly until everything is evenly incorporated. Using your hands, shape the mixture into patties. 4. Place the patties in the refrigerator for about 2 hours to firm up. When ready to cook, air fry the patties for 13 minutes at 395ºF (202ºC). Serve them with some extra English mustard on the side.

Per Serving:
calories: 297 | fat: 16g | protein: 33g | carbs: 5g | net carbs: 4g | fiber: 1g

Steamed Lobster Tails with Thyme

- 4 lobster tails
- 1 tablespoon butter, softened
- 1 teaspoon dried thyme
- 1 cup water

1. Start by pouring water into the Instant Pot and inserting the steamer rack. 2. Place the lobster tails on the rack and securely close the lid. 3. Set the Instant Pot to Manual mode (High Pressure) and cook for 4 minutes. Once the cooking time is complete, perform a quick pressure release. 4. After releasing the pressure, mix together the butter and dried thyme. Peel the lobster tails and generously rub them with the thyme butter before serving. Enjoy!

Per Serving:
calories: 126 | fat: 3g | protein: 24g | carbs: 0g | net carbs: 0g | fiber: 0g

Tuna Patties with Spicy Sriracha Sauce

Prep time: 10 minutes | Cook time: 10 minutes | Serves 4

- 2 (6 ounces / 170 g) cans tuna packed in oil, drained
- 3 tablespoons almond flour
- 2 tablespoons mayonnaise

Spicy Sriracha Sauce:

- ¼ cup mayonnaise
- 1 tablespoon Sriracha sauce

- 1 teaspoon dried dill
- ½ teaspoon onion powder
- Pinch of salt and pepper

- 1 teaspoon garlic powder

1. Preheat your air fryer to 380ºF (193ºC) and line the basket with parchment paper to prevent sticking. 2. In a large mixing bowl, combine the tuna, almond flour, mayonnaise, dill, and onion powder. Season the mixture to taste with salt and freshly ground black pepper. Use a fork to stir the ingredients together, mashing the tuna with the back of the fork as needed until everything is thoroughly combined. 3. Using an ice cream scoop, form the tuna mixture into patties. Place the patties in a single layer on the parchment paper in the air fryer basket. Gently press down on each patty with the bottom of the scoop to flatten them into circles about ½ inch thick. 4. Air fry the patties for a total of 10 minutes, pausing halfway through to turn them for even cooking. They should be lightly browned when done. 5. While the patties are cooking, prepare the Sriracha sauce by combining mayonnaise, Sriracha, and garlic powder in a small bowl. Mix well until smooth. 6. Once the tuna patties are cooked, serve them topped with the Sriracha sauce. Enjoy your delicious and flavorful meal!

Per Serving:
calories: 241 | fat: 15g | protein: 24g | carbs: 2g | net carbs: 1g | fiber: 1g

Pecan-Crusted Catfish

Prep time: 5 minutes | Cook time: 12 minutes | Serves 4

- ½ cup pecan meal
- 1 teaspoon fine sea salt
- ¼ teaspoon ground black

For Garnish (Optional):

- Fresh oregano

- pepper
- 4 (4 ounces / 113 g) catfish fillets

- Pecan halves

1. Begin by spraying the air fryer basket with avocado oil and preheating the air fryer to 375ºF (191ºC). 2. In a large bowl, combine the pecan meal, salt, and pepper. Take each catfish fillet and dredge it in the mixture, ensuring it is well coated. Use your hands to press the pecan meal into the fillets for better adherence. After coating, spray the fish with avocado oil and place them in the air fryer basket. 3. Air fry the coated catfish for 12 minutes, flipping them halfway through, until they flake easily and are no longer translucent in the center. 4. If desired, garnish the cooked catfish with oregano sprigs and pecan halves. 5. To store leftovers, place them in an airtight container in the fridge for up to 3 days. When ready to reheat, use a preheated air fryer set to 350ºF (177ºC) for 4 minutes, or until heated through.

Per Serving:
calories: 390 | fat: 28g | protein: 27g | carbs: 6g | net carbs: 4g | fiber: 2g

Pork Rind Salmon Cakes

Prep time: 10 minutes | Cook time: 10 minutes | Serves 2

- 6 ounces canned Alaska wild salmon, drained
- 2 tablespoons crushed pork rinds
- 1 egg, lightly beaten
- 3 tablespoons mayonnaise,

- divided
- Pink Himalayan salt
- Freshly ground black pepper
- 1 tablespoon ghee
- ½ tablespoon Dijon mustard

1. In a medium bowl, combine the salmon, crushed pork rinds, egg, and 1½ tablespoons of mayonnaise. Season the mixture with pink Himalayan salt and pepper to taste. Mix well until all ingredients are thoroughly combined. 2. Using your hands, form the salmon mixture into patties about the size of hockey pucks or smaller. Make sure to pat the patties firmly to help them hold together. 3. In a medium skillet, melt the ghee over medium-high heat. Once the ghee is hot and sizzling, carefully place the salmon patties in the pan. Cook for about 3 minutes on each side, or until they are golden brown. Once cooked, transfer the patties to a paper towel-lined plate to absorb any excess oil. 4. In a small bowl, mix together the remaining 1½ tablespoons of mayonnaise and the mustard until well combined. 5. Serve the salmon cakes warm with the mayo-mustard dipping sauce on the side. Enjoy your delicious salmon patties!

Per Serving:
calories: 362 | fat: 31g | protein: 24g | carbs: 1g | net carbs: 1g | fiber: 0g

Chapter **6**

Snacks and Appetizers

Crunchy Ranch Dorito Crackers

Prep time: 15 minutes | Cook time: 37 minutes | Serves 7

- 2 cups riced cauliflower, uncooked
- 1½ cups grated Parmesan cheese
- 2 teaspoons ranch seasoning powder
- ⅛ teaspoon salt
- ⅛ teaspoon black pepper

1. Preheat oven to 375°F. 2. In a medium microwave-safe bowl, microwave riced cauliflower 1 minute. Stir and microwave 1 more minute. 3. Let cool and scoop cauliflower onto a clean dish towel. Squeeze out excess water. 4. Return to bowl and add Parmesan, ranch seasoning, salt, and pepper. Mix thoroughly until moist dough is formed. 5. Place the dough on a large piece of parchment paper. Then place a second piece of parchment paper on top of the dough. Use a rolling pin to flatten the dough to the thickness of a Dorito. 6. After the dough is rolled to the desired thickness, remove the top piece of parchment paper and use a pizza cutter to cut the dough into triangle shapes that are roughly the size of Doritos. 7. Transfer the parchment paper with the cut crackers to a baking sheet. Leave enough space between each cracker so they cook evenly and won't stick to nearby crackers during baking. 8. Bake 25 to 35 minutes until golden brown. 9. Let cool and serve.

Per Serving:

calories: 119 | fat: 8g | protein: 11g | carbs: 4g | net carbs: 3g | fiber: 1g

Cheesy Queso Dip

Prep time: 5 minutes | Cook time: 10 minutes | Serves 6

- ½ cup coconut milk
- ½ jalapeño pepper, seeded and diced
- 1 teaspoon minced garlic
- ½ teaspoon onion powder
- 2 ounces goat cheese
- 6 ounces sharp Cheddar cheese, shredded
- ¼ teaspoon cayenne pepper

1. Place a medium pot over medium heat and add the coconut milk, jalapeño, garlic, and onion powder. 2. Bring the liquid to a simmer and then whisk in the goat cheese until smooth. 3. Add the Cheddar cheese and cayenne and whisk until the dip is thick, 30 seconds to 1 minute. 4. Pour into a serving dish and serve with keto crackers or low-carb vegetables.

Per Serving:

calories: 213 | fat: 19g | protein: 10g | carbs: 2g | net carbs: 2g | fiber: 0g

Sweet and Creamy Pepper Poppers

Prep time: 10 minutes | Cook time: 20 minutes | serves 4

- 12 mini sweet peppers
- 1 (8 ounces) package cream cheese, softened
- 5 slices bacon, cooked and crumbled
- 1 green onion, thinly sliced
- ¼ teaspoon ground black pepper

1. Preheat the oven to 400°F. Line a sheet pan with parchment paper. 2. Cut each sweet pepper in half lengthwise, then remove and discard the seeds; set the peppers aside. 3. In a small bowl, mix together the cream cheese, bacon, green onion (reserve some of the slices for garnish, if desired), and black pepper. Spoon the mixture into the sweet pepper halves. 4. Place the stuffed peppers on the lined sheet pan and bake for 20 minutes, until the peppers are tender and the tops are starting to brown. Garnish with the reserved green onion slices, if desired.

Per Serving:

calories: 163 | fat: 12g | protein: 7g | carbs: 5g | net carbs: 4g | fiber: 1g

Grilled Kale Leaves

Prep time: 10 minutes | Cook time: 5 minutes | Serves 4

- ½ cup good-quality olive oil
- 2 teaspoons freshly squeezed lemon juice
- ½ teaspoon garlic powder
- 7 cups large kale leaves, thoroughly washed and patted dry
- Sea salt, for seasoning
- Freshly ground black pepper, for seasoning

1. Preheat the grill. Set the grill to medium-high heat. 2. Mix the dressing. In a large bowl, whisk together the olive oil, lemon juice, and garlic powder until it thickens. 3. Prepare the kale. Add the kale leaves to the bowl and use your fingers to massage the dressing thoroughly all over the leaves. Season the leaves lightly with salt and pepper. 4. Grill and serve. Place the kale leaves in a single layer on the preheated grill. Grill for 1 to 2 minutes, turn the leaves over, and grill the other side for 1 minute, until they're crispy. Put the leaves on a platter and serve.

Per Serving:

calories: 282 | fat: 28g | protein: 3g | carbs: 9g | net carbs: 6g | fiber: 3g

Cajun-Style Coconut Shrimp

Prep time: 10 minutes | Cook time: 6 minutes | Serves 2

- 4 Royal tiger shrimps
- 3 tablespoons coconut shred
- 2 eggs, beaten
- ½ teaspoon Cajun seasoning
- 1 teaspoon olive oil

1. Heat up olive oil in the instant pot on Sauté mode. 2. Meanwhile, mix up Cajun seasoning and coconut shred. 3. Dip the shrimps in the eggs and coat in the coconut shred mixture. 4. After this, place the shrimps in the hot olive oil and cook them on Sauté mode for 3 minutes from each side.

Per Serving:
calories: 292 | fat: 54g | protein: 40g | carbs: 2g | net carbs: 1g | fiber: 1g

Spicy Chicken Tinga Wings

Prep time: 10 minutes | Cook time: 30 minutes | Serves 6

- 1 to 2 cups coconut oil, for frying
- 1 pound (454 g) chicken wings (about 12 wings)

Tinga Sauce:

- 1 pound (454 g) Mexican-style fresh (raw) chorizo
- ½ large white onion, chopped
- 1 clove garlic, minced
- 3 cups chopped tomatoes
- 1 cup chopped husked tomatillos
- 2 tablespoons puréed

- Fine sea salt and freshly ground black pepper, to taste

- chipotles in adobo sauce
- 1½ teaspoons fine sea salt
- 1 teaspoon freshly ground black pepper
- ½ teaspoon dried oregano leaves
- 1 sprig fresh thyme
- ½ cup chicken bone broth, homemade or store-bought

1. Preheat the oil to 350ºF (180ºC) in a deep-fryer or a 4-inch-deep (or deeper) cast-iron skillet over medium heat. The oil should be at least 3 inches deep; add more oil if needed. 2. While the oil heats, make the sauce: Cook the chorizo, onion, and garlic in a large cast-iron skillet over medium heat until the meat is crumbled and cooked through, about 5 minutes. Add the tomatoes, tomatillos, chipotles, salt, pepper, and herbs and stir to combine. Continue cooking for 5 minutes. Add the chicken broth and cook for 5 more minutes. Remove the thyme sprig and set the sauce aside. 3. Fry about six wings at a time until golden brown on all sides and cooked through, about 8 minutes. Remove from the oil and sprinkle with salt and pepper. Repeat with the remaining wings. 4. Place the wings on a serving platter and serve with the sauce, or toss the wings in the sauce before serving. They are best served fresh. Store extra wings and sauce separately in airtight containers in the fridge for up to 3 days. To reheat, place the chicken wings on a rimmed baking sheet and heat in a preheated 400ºF (205ºC) oven for 4 minutes, or until warmed. Heat the sauce in a saucepan over medium-low heat until warmed.

Per Serving:
calories: 247 | fat: 17g | protein: 19g | carbs: 5g | net carbs: 3g | fiber: 2g

Herbed Pickled Herring

Prep time: 4 minutes | Cook time: 5 minutes | Serves 12

- 4 pounds (1.8 kg) herring or skinned Northern Pike fillets, cut into 2-inch pieces

Pickling Brine:

- ½ cup thinly sliced red onions
- Handful of fresh dill
- 2 cups water
- 2½ cups coconut vinegar
- ½ cup Swerve confectioners'-style sweetener or equivalent amount of liquid or

For Serving:

- Hard-boiled eggs, halved or quartered
- Pickled ginger
- Capers

- Saltwater Brine:
- 10 cups water
- ½ cup fine sea salt

- powdered sweetener
- 2 teaspoons ground allspice
- 1 teaspoon dry mustard or mustard seeds
- ½ teaspoon grated fresh ginger
- ½ teaspoon prepared horseradish
- ½ teaspoon peppercorns

- Fermented pickles
- Sliced red onions
- Fresh dill sprigs

1. Place the fish in a large bowl with the 10 cups of water. Add the salt and stir. Cover and refrigerate for 24 hours, then drain the fish and rinse it well. 2. Place the drained and rinsed fish in a clean 2-liter glass jar, layering it with the sliced onions and dill. 3. In a large pot over medium heat, heat the 2 cups of water, coconut vinegar, sweetener, allspice, mustard, ginger, horseradish, and peppercorns. Once the sweetener has dissolved, about 5 minutes, allow the brine to cool a little, then pour over the fish packed in the jar. Cover and refrigerate overnight to allow the flavors to meld; the longer the better for stronger flavors. If you let it sit for 5 days, the bones will dissolve. The pickled fish will keep in an airtight container in the fridge for up to 1 month. 4. To serve, arrange the pickled fish on a platter with hard-boiled eggs, pickled ginger, capers, fermented pickles, sliced red onions, and fresh dill.

Per Serving:
calories: 240 | fat: 14g | protein: 27g | carbs: 2g | net carbs: 2g | fiber: 0g

Crispy Breaded Mushroom Nuggets

Prep time: 15 minutes | Cook time: 50 minutes | Serves 4

- 24 cremini mushrooms (about 1 lb/455 g)
- 2 large eggs
- ½ cup (55 g) blanched almond flour
- 1 teaspoon garlic powder
- 1 teaspoon paprika
- ½ teaspoon finely ground sea salt
- 2 tablespoons avocado oil
- ½ cup (120 ml) honey mustard dressing, for serving (optional)

Special Equipment (optional):

- Toothpicks

1. Preheat the oven to 350°F (177°C). Line a rimmed baking sheet with parchment paper or a silicone baking mat. 2. Break the stems off the mushrooms or cut them short so that the stems are level with the caps. 3. Crack the eggs into a small bowl and whisk. 4. Place the almond flour, garlic powder, paprika, and salt in a medium-sized bowl and whisk to combine. 5. Dip one mushroom at a time into the eggs, then use the same hand to drop it into the flour mixture, being careful not to get the flour mixture on that hand. Rotate the mushroom in the flour mixture with a fork to coat on all sides, then transfer it to the lined baking sheet. Repeat with the remaining mushrooms. 6. Drizzle the coated mushrooms with the oil. Bake for 50 minutes, or until the tops begin to turn golden. 7. Remove from the oven and serve with the dressing, if using. If serving to friends and family, provide toothpicks.

Per Serving:

calories: 332 | fat: 29g | protein: 8g | carbs: 9g | net carbs: 7g | fiber: 2g

Smoky Salmon Fat Bombs

Prep time: 10 minutes | Cook time: 0 minutes | Makes 12 fat bombs

- ½ cup goat cheese, at room temperature
- ½ cup butter, at room temperature
- 2 ounces smoked salmon
- 2 teaspoons freshly squeezed lemon juice
- Pinch freshly ground black pepper

1. Line a baking sheet with parchment paper and set aside. 2. In a medium bowl, stir together the goat cheese, butter, smoked salmon, lemon juice, and pepper until very well blended. 3. Use a tablespoon to scoop the salmon mixture onto the baking sheet until you have 12 even mounds. 4. Place the baking sheet in the refrigerator until the fat bombs are firm, 2 to 3 hours. 5. Store the fat bombs in a sealed container in the refrigerator for up to 1 week.

Per Serving:

2 fat bomb: calories: 193 | fat: 18g | protein: 8g | carbs: 0g | net carbs: 0g | fiber: 0g

Mediterranean-Inspired Fat Bombs

Prep time: 15 minutes | Cook time: 0 minutes | Makes 6 fat bombs

- 1 cup crumbled goat cheese
- 4 tablespoons jarred pesto
- 12 pitted Kalamata olives, finely chopped
- ½ cup finely chopped walnuts
- 1 tablespoon chopped fresh rosemary

1. In a medium bowl, combine the goat cheese, pesto, and olives and mix well using a fork. Place in the refrigerator for at least 4 hours to harden. 2. Using your hands, form the mixture into 6 balls, about ¾-inch diameter. The mixture will be sticky. 3. In a small bowl, place the walnuts and rosemary and roll the goat cheese balls in the nut mixture to coat. 4. Store the fat bombs in the refrigerator for up to 1 week or in the freezer for up to 1 month.

Per Serving:

1 fat bomb: calories: 220 | fat: 20g | protein: 7g | carbs: 4g | net carbs: 3g | fiber: 1g

Oregano Sausage Balls

Prep time: 10 minutes | Cook time: 16 minutes | Serves 10

- 15 ounces (425 g) ground pork sausage
- 1 teaspoon dried oregano
- 4 ounces (113 g) Mozzarella, shredded
- 1 cup coconut flour
- 1 garlic clove, grated
- 1 teaspoon coconut oil, melted

1. In the bowl mix up ground pork sausages, dried oregano, shredded Mozzarella, coconut flour, and garlic clove. 2. When the mixture is homogenous, make the balls. 3. After this, pour coconut oil in the instant pot. 4. Arrange the balls in the instant pot and cook them on Sauté mode for 8 minutes from each side.

Per Serving:

calories: 310 | fat: 23g | protein: 17g | carbs: 10g | net carbs: 5g | fiber: 5g

Turmeric-Infused Cauliflower "Pickles"

Prep time: 10 minutes | Cook time: 5 minutes | serves 6

- 1 cauliflower head, cut into florets
- ⅔ cup white vinegar
- ⅓ cup water
- ½ cup powdered monk fruit sweetener
- 1 tablespoon sea salt
- 1 teaspoon ground coriander
- 1 teaspoon turmeric powder
- 1 bay leaf
- 1 teaspoon peppercorns

1. Place the cauliflower florets in large Mason jars. 2. In a medium saucepan over medium heat, combine the vinegar, water, monk fruit sweetener, salt, coriander, turmeric, bay leaf, and peppercorns. Bring the brine to a low simmer for 5 minutes. Remove the pan from the heat and allow it to cool. 3. Once the brine has cooled, pour it over the cauliflower in the jars. 4. Be sure to fill the jars all the way to the top to ensure that the cauliflower is completely covered. 5. Close the jars to make them as airtight as possible. 6. Store the jars in the refrigerator for 3 days to ferment before eating.

Per Serving:

calories: 26 | fat: 1g | protein: 2g | carbs: 5g | net carbs: 2g | fiber: 3g

Herb-Infused Shrimp

Prep time: 5 minutes | Cook time: 5 minutes | Serves 4

- 2 tablespoons olive oil
- ¾ pound (340 g) shrimp, peeled and deveined
- 1 teaspoon paprika
- 1 teaspoon garlic powder
- 1 teaspoon onion powder
- 1 teaspoon dried parsley flakes
- ½ teaspoon dried oregano
- ½ teaspoon dried thyme
- ½ teaspoon dried basil
- ½ teaspoon dried rosemary
- ¼ teaspoon red pepper flakes
- Coarse sea salt and ground black pepper, to taste
- 1 cup chicken broth

1. Set your Instant Pot to Sauté and heat the olive oil. 2. Add the shrimp and sauté for 2 to 3 minutes. 3. Add the remaining ingredients to the Instant Pot and stir to combine. 4. Secure the lid. Select the Manual mode and set the cooking time for 2 minutes at Low Pressure. 5. When the timer beeps, perform a quick pressure release. Carefully remove the lid. 6. Transfer the shrimp to a plate and serve.

Per Serving:

calories: 146 | fat: 8g | protein: 19g | carbs: 3g | net carbs: 2g | fiber: 1g

Creamy Cheese with Fresh Berries

Prep time: 5 minutes | Cook time: 0 minutes | Serves 1

- 2 ounces (57 g) cream cheese
- 2 large strawberries, cut into
- thin slices or chunks
- 5 blueberries
- ⅛ cup chopped pecans

1. Place the cream cheese on a small plate or in a bowl. 2. Pour the berries and chopped pecans on top. Enjoy!

Per Serving:

calories: 330 | fat: 31g | protein: 6g | carbs: 7g | net carbs: 5g | fiber: 2g

Low-Carb Fathead Crackers

Prep time: 10 minutes | Cook time: 10 minutes | Serves 8

- 1½ cups shredded mozzarella cheese (about 6 ounces)
- 2 ounces cream cheese (¼ cup)
- 1 cup blanched almond flour
- 1 large egg
- ½ teaspoon dried parsley
- ½ teaspoon pink Himalayan salt

1. Preheat the oven to 425°F and line a baking sheet with parchment paper. 2. Put the mozzarella and cream cheese in a large microwave-safe mixing bowl and microwave for 30 seconds. Combine using a rubber spatula. Microwave for another 30 seconds, until the cheese has melted, then stir once more. 3. Add the almond flour, egg, parsley, and salt and, using a fork, combine everything thoroughly until you have a soft, sticky, and pliable dough. 4. Once the dough comes together, transfer it to the lined baking sheet and place another piece of parchment paper on top. Roll out into a thin rectangle, about ¼ inch thick. Using a pizza cutter or knife, cut the flattened dough into 20 to 25 small crackers, about 1 inch. 5. Discard any extra dough and spread out the crackers so they are not touching one another. Bake for 7 to 10 minutes, until the crackers have puffed up and browned. Allow to cool on the baking sheet for 10 minutes prior to eating. 6. These are best eaten the same day they are baked, but leftovers can be stored in a sealed container in the refrigerator for up to 5 days. To recrisp, place in a preheated 250°F oven for 5 minutes; however, they will not get as crispy as when freshly baked.

Per Serving:

calories: 174 | fat: 15g | protein: 9g | carbs: 4g | net carbs: 2g | fiber: 2g

Elegant Crudités with Dipping Sauce

Prep time: 15 minutes | Cook time: 0 minutes | Serves 8

- ♦ Vegetables
- ♦ 1 cup whole cherry tomatoes
- ♦ 1 cup green beans, trimmed
- ♦ 2 cups broccoli florets
- ♦ 2 cups cauliflower florets
- ♦ 1 bunch asparagus, trimmed
- ♦ 1 large green bell pepper, seeded and chopped
- ♦ Sour Cream Dip
- ♦ 2 cups full-fat sour cream
- ♦ 3 tablespoons dry chives
- ♦ 1 tablespoon lemon juice
- ♦ ½ cup dried parsley
- ♦ ½ teaspoon garlic powder
- ♦ ⅛ teaspoon salt
- ♦ ⅛ teaspoon black pepper

1. Cut vegetables into bite-sized uniform pieces. Arrange in like groups around outside edge of a large serving platter, leaving room in middle for dip. 2. Make dip by combining dip ingredients in a medium-sized decorative bowl and mixing well. 3. Place dip bowl in the center of platter and serve.

Per Serving:
calories: 146| fat: 10g | protein: 4g | carbs: 9g | net carbs: 6g | fiber: 3g

Power-Packed Fat Bombs

Prep time: 10 minutes | Cook time: 0 minutes | Makes 8 bombs

- ♦ ⅔ cup (145 g) coconut oil, cacao butter, or ghee, melted
- ♦ ¼ cup (40 g) collagen peptides or protein powder
- ♦ ¼ cup (25 g) unflavored MCT oil powder
- ♦ 2 tablespoons cocoa powder
- ♦ 2 tablespoons roughly ground flax seeds
- ♦ 1 tablespoon cacao nibs
- ♦ 1 teaspoon instant coffee granules
- ♦ 4 drops liquid stevia, or 1 tablespoon plus 1 teaspoon confectioners'-style erythritol
- ♦ Pinch of finely ground sea salt

Special Equipment (Optional):

- ♦ Silicone mold with eight 2-tablespoon or larger cavities

1. Have on hand your favorite silicone mold. I like to use a large silicone ice cube tray and spoon 2 tablespoons of the mixture into each well, If you do not have a silicone mold, making this into a bark works well, too. Simply use an 8-inch (20 cm) square silicone or metal baking pan; if using a metal pan, line it with parchment paper, draping some over the sides for easy removal. 2. Place all the ingredients in a medium-sized bowl and stir until well mixed and smooth. 3. Divide the mixture evenly among 8 cavities in the silicone mold or pour into the baking pan. Transfer to the fridge and allow to set for 15 minutes if using cacao butter or 30 minutes if using ghee or coconut oil. If using a baking pan, break the bark into 8 pieces for serving.

Per Serving:
calories: 136 | fat: 12g | protein: 6g | carbs: 3g | net carbs: 1g | fiber: 2g

Spiced Curried Broccoli Skewers

Prep time: 15 minutes | Cook time: 1 minute | Serves 2

- ♦ 1 cup broccoli florets
- ♦ ½ teaspoon curry paste
- ♦ 2 tablespoons coconut cream
- ♦ 1 cup water, for cooking

1. In the shallow bowl mix up curry paste and coconut cream. 2. Then sprinkle the broccoli florets with curry paste mixture and string on the skewers. 3. Pour water and insert the steamer rack in the instant pot. 4. Place the broccoli skewers on the rack. Close and seal the lid. 5. Cook the meal on Manual mode (High Pressure) for 1 minute. 6. Make a quick pressure release.

Per Serving:
calories: 58 | fat: 4g | protein: 2g | carbs: 4g | net carbs: 2g | fiber: 2g

Herb-Seasoned Rosemary Chicken Wings

Prep time: 10 minutes | Cook time: 16 minutes | Serves 4

- ♦ 4 boneless chicken wings
- ♦ 1 tablespoon olive oil
- ♦ 1 teaspoon dried rosemary
- ♦ ½ teaspoon garlic powder
- ♦ ¼ teaspoon salt

1. In the mixing bowl, mix up olive oil, dried rosemary, garlic powder, and salt. 2. Then rub the chicken wings with the rosemary mixture and leave for 10 minutes to marinate. 3. After this, put the chicken wings in the instant pot, add the remaining rosemary marinade and cook them on Sauté mode for 8 minutes from each side.

Per Serving:
calories: 222 | fat: 11g | protein: 27g | carbs: 2g | net carbs: 2g | fiber: 0g

Edana's Macadamia Crunch Bars

Prep time: 15 minutes | Cook time: 35 minutes | Makes 12 bars

Base:

- 1¼ cups (140 g) blanched almond flour
- ⅓ cup (65 g) erythritol
- ⅓ cup (70 g) coconut oil, ghee, or cacao butter,

Coconut Cream Layer:

- ½ cup (95 g) erythritol
- ½ cup (125 g) coconut cream
- ¼ cup (55 g) coconut oil,

Toppings:

- 1 cup (160 g) raw macadamia nuts, roughly chopped

- melted
- 1 teaspoon vanilla extract
- ¼ teaspoon finely ground sea salt

- ghee, or cacao butter, melted
- 2 large egg yolks
- 1 teaspoon vanilla extract

- 1 cup (100 g) unsweetened shredded coconut

1. Preheat the oven to 350°F (177°C). Line an 8-inch (20 cm) square baking pan with parchment paper, draping it over two opposite sides of the pan for easy lifting. 2. Place the base ingredients in a large mixing bowl and stir to combine. Press into the prepared pan and par-bake for 10 to 12 minutes, until the top is only lightly browned. Remove from the oven and lower the oven temperature to 300°F (150°C). 3. Meanwhile, make the coconut cream layer: Place the erythritol, coconut cream, melted oil, egg yolks, and vanilla in a large mixing bowl. Whisk until smooth. 4. Pour the coconut cream mixture over the par-baked base. Top with the macadamia nuts, then the shredded coconut. 5. Return the pan to the oven and bake for 25 minutes, or until the edges are lightly browned. 6. Let cool in the pan on the counter for 1 hour before transferring to the fridge to chill for another hour. Once chilled, cut into 2-inch (5 cm) squares.

Per Serving:

calories: 303 | fat: 31g | protein: 2g | carbs: 6g | net carbs: 2g | fiber: 3g

Sliced Artichokes

Prep time: 5 minutes | Cook time: 35 minutes | Serves 4

- ½ teaspoon salt, divided
- 2 large artichokes, trimmed

- 2 tablespoons lemon juice
- ½ cup full-fat mayonnaise

1. In a large pot, prepare 1" water with ¼ teaspoon salt. 2. Put artichokes in a steamer basket inside pot, stem-side up, and cover pot. When boiling starts, reduce heat to medium-low and leave untouched 25 minutes. 3. Test to see if done by pulling off outer leaf using tongs. If it doesn't come off easily, add additional water to pot and steam 5–10 more minutes. Let cool. 4. Serve with dip made by combining lemon juice, mayonnaise, and remaining salt.

Per Serving:

calories: 219 | fat: 20g | protein: 2g | carbs: 8g | net carbs: 3g | fiber: 5g

Low-Carb Asian-Style Dumplings

Prep time: 20 minutes | Cook time: 20 minutes | Serves 4

Dipping Sauce:

- ¼ cup gluten-free soy sauce
- 2 tablespoons sesame oil

Filling:

- 1 tablespoon sesame oil
- 2 garlic cloves
- 1 teaspoon grated fresh ginger
- 1 celery stalk, minced
- ½ onion, minced
- 1 carrot, minced
- 8 ounces (227 g) ground pork
- 8 ounces (227 g) shrimp, peeled, deveined, and finely

- 1 tablespoon rice vinegar
- 1 teaspoon chili garlic sauce

- chopped
- 2 tablespoons gluten-free soy sauce
- ½ teaspoon fish sauce
- Salt and freshly ground black pepper, to taste
- 3 scallions, green parts only, chopped
- 1 head napa cabbage, rinsed, leaves separated (about 12 leaves)

Make the Dipping Sauce 1. In a small bowl, whisk together the soy sauce, sesame oil, vinegar, and chili garlic sauce. Set aside. Make the Filling 2. In a large skillet over medium heat, heat the sesame oil. 3. Add the garlic, ginger, celery, onion, and carrot. Sauté for 5 to 7 minutes until softened. 4. Add the pork. Cook for 5 to 6 minutes, breaking it up with a spoon, until it starts to brown. 5. Add the shrimp and stir everything together well. 6. Stir in the soy sauce and fish sauce. Season with a little salt and pepper. Give it a stir and add the scallions. Keep it warm over low heat until ready to fill the dumplings. 7. Steam the cabbage leaves: Place the leaves in a large saucepan with just 1 to 2 inches of boiling water. Cook for about 5 minutes or until the leaves become tender. Remove from the water and set aside to drain. 8. Lay each leaf out flat. Put about 2 tablespoons of filling in the center of one leaf. Wrap the leaf over itself, tucking the sides in so the whole thing is tightly wrapped. Secure with a toothpick. Continue with the remaining leaves and filling. Serve with the dipping sauce. Refrigerate leftovers in an airtight container for up to 3 days.

Per Serving:

3 dumplings: calories: 305 | fat: 17g | protein: 27g | carbs: 11g | net carbs: 8g | fiber: 3g

Bacon-Infused Pimento Cheese

Prep time: 10 minutes | Cook time: 5 minutes | Serves 6

- 2 ounces (57 g) bacon (about 4 thick slices)
- 4 ounces (113 g) cream cheese, room temperature
- ¼ cup mayonnaise
- ¼ teaspoon onion powder
- ¼ teaspoon cayenne pepper (optional)
- 1 cup thick-shredded extra-sharp Cheddar cheese
- 2 ounces (57 g) jarred diced pimentos, drained

1. Chop the raw bacon into ½-inch-thick pieces. Cook in a small skillet over medium heat until crispy, 3 to 4 minutes. Use a slotted spoon to transfer the bacon onto a layer of paper towels. Reserve the rendered fat. 2. In a large bowl, combine the cream cheese, mayonnaise, onion powder, and cayenne (if using), and beat with an electric mixer or by hand until smooth and creamy. 3. Add the rendered bacon fat, Cheddar cheese, and pimentos and mix until well combined. 4. Refrigerate for at least 30 minutes before serving to allow flavors to blend. Serve cold with raw veggies.

Per Serving:

calories: 216 | fat: 20g | protein: 8g | carbs: 2g | net carbs: 0g | fiber: 2

Zesty Lemon-Pepper Chicken Drumsticks

Prep time: 30 minutes | Cook time: 30 minutes | Serves 2

- 2 teaspoons freshly ground coarse black pepper
- 1 teaspoon baking powder
- ½ teaspoon garlic powder
- 4 chicken drumsticks (4 ounces / 113 g each)
- Kosher salt, to taste
- 1 lemon

1. In a small bowl, stir together the pepper, baking powder, and garlic powder. Place the drumsticks on a plate and sprinkle evenly with the baking powder mixture, turning the drumsticks so they're well coated. Let the drumsticks stand in the refrigerator for at least 1 hour or up to overnight. 2. Sprinkle the drumsticks with salt, then transfer them to the air fryer, standing them bone-end up and leaning against the wall of the air fryer basket. Air fry at 375°F (191°C) until cooked through and crisp on the outside, about 30 minutes. 3. Transfer the drumsticks to a serving platter and finely grate the zest of the lemon over them while they're hot. Cut the lemon into wedges and serve with the warm drumsticks.

Per Serving:

calories: 200 | fat: 9g | protein: 28g | carbs: 5g | net carbs: 4g | fiber: 1g

Chia Pudding with Almonds and Chocolate

Prep time: 10 minutes | Cook time: 0 minutes | Serves 4

- 1 (14 ounces / 397 g) can full-fat coconut milk
- ⅓ cup chia seeds
- 1 tablespoon unsweetened cocoa powder
- 2 tablespoons unsweetened almond butter
- 2 to 3 teaspoons granulated sugar-free sweetener of choice (optional)
- ½ teaspoon vanilla extract
- ½ teaspoon almond extract (optional)

1. Combine all the ingredients in a small bowl, whisking well to fully incorporate the almond butter. 2. Divide the mixture between four ramekins or small glass jars. 3. Cover and refrigerate for at least 6 hours, preferably overnight. Serve cold.

Per Serving:

calories: 335 | fat: 31g | protein: 7g | carbs: 13g | net carbs: 6g | fiber: 7g

Low-Carb Taco Shells

Prep time: 5 minutes | Cook time: 20 minutes | Serves 4

6 ounces (170 g) shredded cheese

1. Preheat the oven to 350°F (180°C). 2. Line a baking sheet with a silicone baking mat or parchment paper. 3. Separate the cheese into 4 (1½-ounce / 43-g) portions and make small circular piles a few inches apart (they will spread a bit in the oven). Pat the cheese down so all the piles are equally thick. Bake for 10 to 12 minutes or until the edges begin to brown. Cool for just a couple of minutes. 4. Lay a wooden spoon or spatula across two overturned glasses. Repeat to make a second setup, and carefully transfer a baked cheese circle to drape over the length of each spoon or spatula. Let them cool into the shape of a taco shell. 5. Fill with your choice of protein and top with chopped lettuce, avocado, salsa, sour cream, or whatever else you like on your tacos. These taco shells will keep refrigerated in an airtight container for a few days, but they are best freshly made and still a little warm.

Per Serving:

1 taco shell: calories: 168 | fat: 14g | protein: 11g | carbs: 1g | net carbs: 1g | fiber: 0g

Crispy Cheddar Chips

Prep time: 10 minutes | Cook time: 5 minutes | Serves 4

- 1 cup shredded Cheddar cheese
- 1 tablespoon almond flour

1. Mix up Cheddar cheese and almond flour. 2. Then preheat the instant pot on Sauté mode. 3. Line the instant pot bowl with baking paper. 4. After this, make the small rounds from the cheese in the instant pot (on the baking paper) and close the lid. 5. Cook them for 5 minutes on Sauté mode or until the cheese is melted. 6. Then switch off the instant pot and remove the baking paper with cheese rounds from it. 7. Cool the chips well and remove them from the baking paper.

Per Serving:

calories: 154 | fat: 13g | protein: 9g | carbs: 2g | net carbs: 1g | fiber: 1g

Hearty Mac Fatties

Prep time: 10 minutes | Cook time: 0 minutes | Makes 20 fat cups

- 1¾ cups (280 g) roasted and salted macadamia nuts
Rosemary Lemon Flavor:
- 1 teaspoon finely chopped fresh rosemary
Spicy Cumin Flavor:
- ½ teaspoon ground cumin
Turmeric Flavor:
- ½ teaspoon turmeric powder
Garlic Herb Flavor:
- 1¼ teaspoons dried oregano leaves

- ⅓ cup (70 g) coconut oil

- ¼ teaspoon lemon juice

- ¼ teaspoon cayenne pepper

- ¼ teaspoon ginger powder

- ½ teaspoon paprika
- ½ teaspoon garlic powder

1. Place the macadamia nuts and oil in a blender or food processor. Blend until smooth, or as close to smooth as you can get it with the equipment you're using. 2. Divide the mixture among 4 small bowls, placing ¼ cup (87 g) in each bowl. 3. To the first bowl, add the rosemary and lemon juice and stir to combine. 4. To the second bowl, add the cumin and cayenne and stir to combine. 5. To the third bowl, add the turmeric and ginger and stir to combine. 6. To the fourth bowl, add the oregano, paprika, and garlic powder and stir to combine. 7. Set a 24-well silicone or metal mini muffin pan on the counter. If using a metal pan, line 20 of the wells with mini foil liners. (Do not use paper; it would soak up all the fat.) Spoon the mixtures into the wells, using about 1 tablespoon per well. 8.

Place in the freezer for 1 hour, or until firm. Enjoy directly from the freezer.

Per Serving:

calories: 139 | fat: 14g | protein: 1g | carbs: 2g | net carbs: 1g | fiber: 1g

Signature EL Presidente Guacamole

Prep time: 10 minutes | Cook time: 0 minutes | Serves 4

- 2 large avocados, peeled and pitted
- 1 tablespoon garlic powder
- 1 tablespoon onion powder
- ⅛ teaspoon salt

- ⅛ teaspoon chili powder
- 4 tablespoons finely chopped cilantro
- 1 Roma tomato, finely chopped
- 4 teaspoons lime juice

1. In a medium bowl, mash avocados and combine with dry spices. 2. Add cilantro, tomato, and lime juice and mix again. Serve.

Per Serving:

calories: 131| fat: 9g | protein: 2g | carbs: 10g | net carbs: 5g | fiber: 5g

Zesty Citrus-Marinated Olives

Prep time: 10 minutes | Cook time: 0 minutes | Makes 2 cups

- 2 cups mixed green olives with pits
- ¼ cup red wine vinegar
- ¼ cup extra-virgin olive oil
- 4 garlic cloves, finely minced
- Zest and juice of 2

- clementines or 1 large orange
- 1 teaspoon red pepper flakes
- 2 bay leaves
- ½ teaspoon ground cumin
- ½ teaspoon ground allspice

1. In a large glass bowl or jar, combine the olives, vinegar, oil, garlic, orange zest and juice, red pepper flakes, bay leaves, cumin, and allspice and mix well. Cover and refrigerate for at least 4 hours or up to a week to allow the olives to marinate, tossing again before serving.

Per Serving:

¼ cup: calories: 100 | fat: 10g | protein: 1g | carbs: 3g | net carbs: 2g | fiber: 1g

Toasted Coconut Chips with Vanilla

Prep time: 5 minutes | Cook time: 10 minutes | Serves 8

- 1 tablespoon coconut oil, melted
- 2 tablespoons powdered erythritol
- ½ teaspoon vanilla extract
- Pinch of sea salt
- 2 cups unsweetened coconut chips (no other ingredients added)

1. Preheat the oven to 325°F (163°C). Line a baking sheet with parchment paper. 2. In a medium bowl, whisk together the melted coconut oil, powdered erythritol, vanilla, and sea salt. It may clump, which is okay. Add the coconut chips and toss to coat. 3. Arrange the coconut chips in a single layer on the baking sheet. Bake for about 5 minutes, or until some pieces are starting to turn golden. Stir, then bake for another 3 to 5 minutes, until more golden. 4. Cool completely to crisp up; they will not be crisp right out of the oven.

Per Serving:

calories: 155 | fat: 15g | protein: 1g | carbs: 7g | net carbs: 2g | fiber: 5g

Flavorful Marinated Cheese

Prep time: 10 minutes | Cook time: 0 minutes | Serves 8

- ½ cup olive oil
- ½ cup white wine vinegar
- 2 or 3 garlic cloves, minced
- 4 scallions, green parts only, thinly sliced
- 3 tablespoons chopped fresh parsley leaves
- 1 (2-ounce / 57-g) jar diced pimientos, drained
- Salt and freshly ground
- black pepper, to taste
- 1 (8-ounce / 227-g) block sharp Cheddar cheese, halved lengthwise and cut widthwise into ½-inch squares
- 1 (8-ounce / 227-g) block cream cheese halved lengthwise and cut widthwise into ½-inch squares

1. In a small bowl, whisk together the olive oil, vinegar, garlic, scallions, parsley, pimientos, and season with some salt and pepper. 2. In a container with a lid, assemble the cheese (we like to alternate pieces of Cheddar and cream cheese for a prettier presentation) and cover with the marinade. Cover and refrigerate for at least 8 hours. 3. Remove from the refrigerator 15 to 20 minutes before serving, and transfer the cheese to a serving platter, pouring the marinade over the top. Refrigerate leftovers in an airtight container for up to 1 week.

Per Serving:

calories: 336 | fat: 32g | protein: 10g | carbs: 2g | net carbs: 1g | fiber: 1g

Prosciutto-Wrapped Asparagus Bundles

Prep time: 5 minutes | Cook time: 12 minutes | Serves 6

- 18 asparagus spears, ends trimmed
- 2 tablespoons coconut oil,
- melted
- 6 slices prosciutto
- 1 teaspoon garlic powder

1. Preheat the oven to 400°F. Line a rimmed baking sheet with parchment paper. 2. Place the asparagus and coconut oil in a large zip-top plastic bag. Seal and toss until the asparagus is evenly coated. 3. Wrap a slice of prosciutto around 3 grouped asparagus spears. Repeat with the remaining prosciutto and asparagus, making a total of 6 bundles. Arrange the bundles in a single layer on the lined baking sheet. Sprinkle the garlic powder over the bundles. 4. Bake for 8 to 12 minutes, until the asparagus is tender.

Per Serving:

calories: 122 | fat: 10g | protein: 8g | carbs: 3g | net carbs: 2g | fiber: 1g

Pesto-Stuffed Mushrooms

Prep time: 20 minutes | Cook time: 20 minutes | Makes 1 dozen mushrooms

- 1 dozen baby bella mushroom caps, cleaned
- 8 ounces (227 g) fresh Mozzarella
- ½ cup pesto
- Sea salt and ground black pepper, to taste

1. Preheat the oven to 350°F (180°C). 2. Place the mushrooms on a rimmed baking sheet cup side down and bake for 10 minutes, or until some of the moisture is released. 3. While the mushrooms are baking, slice the Mozzarella into small pieces, approximately the size of the mushrooms. 4. Turn the mushrooms cup side up and fill each one with a spoonful of pesto and 1 or 2 pieces of Mozzarella. Return the mushrooms to the oven and bake for about 10 minutes, until golden brown on top. 5. Sprinkle with salt and pepper before serving.

Per Serving:

calories: 132 | fat: 11g | protein: 4g | carbs: 5g | net carbs: 4g | fiber: 1g

Shrimp-Stuffed Bok Choy Salad Boats

Prep time: 8 minutes | Cook time: 2 minutes | Serves 8

- 26 shrimp, cleaned and deveined
- 2 tablespoons fresh lemon juice
- 1 cup water
- Sea salt and ground black pepper, to taste
- 4 ounces (113 g) feta cheese, crumbled
- 2 tomatoes, diced
- ⅓ cup olives, pitted and sliced
- 4 tablespoons olive oil
- 2 tablespoons apple cider vinegar
- 8 Bok choy leaves
- 2 tablespoons fresh basil leaves, snipped
- 2 tablespoons chopped fresh mint leaves

1. Toss the shrimp and lemon juice in the Instant Pot until well coated. Pour in the water. 2. Lock the lid. Select the Manual mode and set the cooking time for 2 minutes at Low Pressure. 3. When the timer beeps, perform a quick pressure release. Carefully remove the lid. 4. Season the shrimp with salt and pepper to taste, then let them cool completely. 5. Toss the shrimp with the feta cheese, tomatoes, olives, olive oil, and vinegar until well incorporated. 6. Divide the salad evenly onto each Bok choy leaf and place them on a serving plate. Scatter the basil and mint leaves on top and serve immediately.

Per Serving:

calories: 129 | fat: 11g | protein: 5g | carbs: 3g | net carbs: 2g | fiber: 1g

Flaky Cheesy Spinach Puffs

Prep time: 10 minutes | Cook time: 10 minutes | Serves 8

- 16 ounces (454 g) frozen spinach, thawed, drained, and squeezed of as much excess liquid as possible
- 1 cup almond flour
- 4 tablespoons butter, melted, plus more for the baking sheet
- 2 eggs
- ¼ cup grated Parmesan cheese
- ¼ cup cream cheese
- 3 tablespoons heavy (whipping) cream
- 1 tablespoon onion powder
- 1 teaspoon garlic powder
- Salt and freshly ground black pepper, to taste

1. In a food processor, combine the spinach, almond flour, butter, eggs, Parmesan, cream cheese, cream, onion powder, and garlic powder. Season with salt and pepper. Blend until smooth. Transfer to the refrigerator and chill for 10 to 15 minutes. 2. Preheat the oven to 350°F (180°C). 3. Grease a baking sheet with butter. 4. Scoop the spinach mixture in heaping tablespoons and roll into balls. Place on the prepared baking sheet and bake for about 10 minutes until set. When tapped with your finger, they should not still be soft. Enjoy warm (best!) or cold. Refrigerate in an airtight container for up to 4 days.

Per Serving:

calories: 159 | fat: 14g | protein: 6g | carbs: 3g | net carbs: 1g | fiber: 2g

Fresh and Easy Quick Salsa

Prep time: 5 minutes | Cook time: 0 minutes | Makes about 3 cups

- ¼ cup fresh cilantro, stems and leaves, finely chopped
- 1 small red onion, finely chopped
- 8 roma tomatoes or other small to medium tomatoes, finely chopped
- 1 small jalapeño pepper, minced, seeded if desired for less heat (optional)
- Juice of 1 to 2 limes
- Sea salt and ground black pepper, to taste

1. Toss together all the ingredients in a large mixing bowl. Alternatively, place all the ingredients in a food processor and pulse until the desired consistency is reached. 2. Season with salt and pepper to taste. 3. Store in an airtight container in the refrigerator for up to 5 days.

Per Serving:

calories: 12 | fat: 3g | protein: 1g | carbs: 3g | net carbs: 2g | fiber 1g

Strawberry Shortcake Coconut Sorbet

Prep time: 5 minutes | Cook time: 0 minutes | Serves 5

- 9 hulled strawberries (fresh or frozen and defrosted)
- ⅓ cup (85 g) coconut cream
- 1 tablespoon apple cider
- vinegar
- 2 drops liquid stevia, or 2 teaspoons erythritol
- 3 cups (420 g) ice cubes

1. Place the strawberries, coconut cream, vinegar, and sweetener in a blender or food processor. Blend until smooth. 2. Add the ice and pulse until crushed. 3. Divide among four ¾-cup (180-ml) or larger bowls and serve immediately.

Per Serving:

calories: 61 | fat: 5g | protein: 0g | carbs: 3g | net carbs: 2g | fiber: 1g

Rich and Creamy Scallion Dip

Prep time: 10 minutes | Cook time: 11 minutes | Serves 4

- 5 ounces (142 g) scallions, diced
- 4 tablespoons cream cheese
- 1 tablespoon chopped fresh parsley
- 1 teaspoon garlic powder
- 2 tablespoons coconut cream
- ½ teaspoon salt
- 1 teaspoon coconut oil

1. Heat up the instant pot on Sauté mode. 2. Then add coconut oil and melt it. 3. Add diced scallions and sauté it for 6 to 7 minutes or until it is light brown. 4. Add cream cheese, parsley, garlic powder, salt, and coconut cream. 5. Close the instant pot lid and cook the scallions dip for 5 minutes on Manual mode (High Pressure). 6. Make a quick pressure release. Blend the dip will it is smooth if desired.

Per Serving:

calories: 76 | fat: 6g | protein: 2g | carbs: 4g | net carbs: 3g | fiber: 1g

Creamy Broccoli Cheese Dip

Prep time: 5 minutes | Cook time: 10 minutes | Serves 6

- 4 tablespoons butter
- ½ medium onion, diced
- 1½ cups chopped broccoli
- 8 ounces (227 g) cream cheese
- ½ cup mayonnaise
- ½ cup chicken broth
- 1 cup shredded Cheddar cheese

1. Press the Sauté button and then press the Adjust button to set heat to Less. Add butter to Instant Pot. Add onion and sauté until softened, about 5 minutes. Press the Cancel button. 2. Add broccoli, cream cheese, mayo, and broth to pot. Press the Manual button and adjust time for 4 minutes. 3. When timer beeps, quick-release the pressure and stir in Cheddar. Serve warm.

Per Serving:

calories: 411 | fat: 37g | protein: 8g | carbs: 4g | net carbs: 3g | fiber: 1g

Flavorful Chinese Spare Ribs

Prep time: 3 minutes | Cook time: 24 minutes | Serves 6

- 1½ pounds (680 g) spare ribs
- Salt and ground black pepper, to taste
- 2 tablespoons sesame oil
- ½ cup chopped green onions
- ½ cup chicken stock
- 2 tomatoes, crushed
- 2 tablespoons sherry
- 1 tablespoon coconut aminos
- 1 teaspoon ginger-garlic paste
- ½ teaspoon crushed red pepper flakes
- ½ teaspoon dried parsley
- 2 tablespoons sesame seeds, for serving

1. Season the spare ribs with salt and black pepper to taste. 2. Set your Instant Pot to Sauté and heat the sesame oil. 3. Add the seasoned spare ribs and sear each side for about 3 minutes. 4. Add the remaining ingredients except the sesame seeds to the Instant Pot and stir well. 5. Secure the lid. Select the Meat/Stew mode and set the cooking time for 18 minutes at High Pressure. 6. When the timer beeps, perform a natural pressure release for 10 minutes, then release any remaining pressure. Carefully remove the lid. 7. Serve topped with the sesame seeds.

Per Serving:

calories: 336 | fat: 16g | protein: 43g | carbs: 3g | net carbs: 2g | fiber: 1g

Finger Tacos with Avocado

Prep time: 15 minutes | Cook time: 0 minutes | serves 4

- 2 avocados, peeled and pitted
- 1 lime
- 1 tablespoon tamari
- 1 teaspoon sesame oil
- 1 teaspoon ginger powder
- 1 teaspoon togarashi (optional)
- ½ cup kale chiffonade
- ½ cup cabbage chiffonade
- 10 fresh mint leaves chiffonade
- ⅓ cup cauliflower rice
- 1 (0.18-ounce) package nori squares or seaweed snack sheets

1. Put the avocados into a large mixing bowl, and squeeze the lime over them. 2. Roughly mash the avocados with a fork, leaving the mixture fairly chunky. 3. Gently stir in the tamari, sesame oil, ginger powder, and togarashi (if using). 4. Gently fold in the kale, cabbage, mint, and cauliflower rice. 5. Arrange some nori squares on a plate. 6. Use a nori or seaweed sheet to pick up a portion of the avocado mixture and pop it into your mouth.

Per Serving:

calories: 180 | fat: 15g | protein: 4g | carbs: 13g | net carbs: 5g | fiber: 8g

Cheesy Cauliflower Fritters

Prep time: 10 minutes | Cook time: 8 minutes | Serves 4

- 1 cup cauliflower, boiled
- 2 eggs, beaten
- 2 tablespoons almond flour
- 2 ounces (57 g) Cheddar cheese, shredded
- ½ teaspoon garlic powder
- 1 tablespoon avocado oil

1. In a medium bowl, mash the cauliflower. Add the beaten eggs, flour, cheese, and garlic powder and stir until well incorporated. Make the fritters from the cauliflower mixture. 2. Set your Instant Pot to Sauté and heat the avocado oil. 3. Add the fritters to the hot oil and cook each side for 3 minutes until golden brown. 4. Serve hot.

Per Serving:
calories: 125 | fat: 10g | protein: 8g | carbs: 3g | net carbs: 1g | fiber: 1g

Delightful Jelly Cups

Prep time: 10 minutes | Cook time: 10 minutes | Makes 16 jelly cups

Butter Base:
- ⅔ cup (170 g) coconut butter or smooth unsweetened nut or seed butter
- ⅔ cup (145 g) coconut oil, ghee, or cacao butter, melted
- 2 teaspoons vanilla extract
- 7 drops liquid stevia, or 2 teaspoons confectioners'-style erythritol

Jelly Filling:
- ½ cup (70 g) fresh raspberries
- ¼ cup (60 ml) water
- 3 drops liquid stevia, or 1 teaspoon confectioners'-style erythritol
- 1½ teaspoons unflavored gelatin

Special Equipment:
- 16 mini muffin cup liners, or 1 silicone mini muffin pan

1. Set 16 mini muffin cup liners on a tray or have on hand a silicone mini muffin pan. 2. Make the base: Place the coconut butter, melted oil, vanilla, and sweetener in a medium-sized bowl and stir to combine. 3. Take half of the base mixture and divide it equally among the 16 mini muffin cup liners or 16 wells of the mini muffin pan, filling each about one-quarter full. Place the muffin cup liners (or muffin pan) in the fridge. Set the remaining half of the base mixture aside. 4. Make the jelly filling: Place the raspberries, water, and sweetener in a small saucepan and bring to a simmer over medium heat. Simmer for 5 minutes, then sprinkle with the gelatin and mash with a fork. Transfer to the fridge to set for 15 minutes. 5. Pull the muffin cup liners and jelly filling out of the fridge. Using

a ½-teaspoon measuring spoon, scoop out a portion of the jelly and roll it into a ball between your palms, then flatten it into a disc about 1 inch (2.5 cm) in diameter (or in a diameter to fit the size of the liners you're using). Press into a chilled butter base cup. Repeat with the remaining jelly filling and cups. Then spoon the remaining butter base mixture over the tops. 6. Place in the fridge for another 15 minutes before serving.

Per Serving:
calories: 151 | fat: 15g | protein: 1g | carbs: 3g | net carbs: 1g | fiber: 2g

Savory Cauliflower Patties

Prep time: 10 minutes | Cook time: 10 minutes | Makes 10 patties

- 1 medium head cauliflower (about 1½ pounds/680 g), or 3 cups (375 g) pre-riced cauliflower
- 2 large eggs
- ⅔ cup (75 g) blanched almond flour
- ¼ cup (17 g) nutritional yeast
- 1 tablespoon dried chives
- 1 teaspoon finely ground sea salt
- 1 teaspoon garlic powder
- ½ teaspoon turmeric powder
- ¼ teaspoon ground black pepper
- 3 tablespoons coconut oil or ghee, for the pan

1. If you're using pre-riced cauliflower, skip ahead to Step 2. Otherwise, cut the base off the head of cauliflower and remove the florets. Transfer the florets to a food processor or blender and pulse 3 or 4 times to break them up into small (¼-inch/6-mm) pieces. 2. Transfer the riced cauliflower to a medium-sized saucepan and add enough water to the pan to completely cover the cauliflower. Cover with the lid and bring to a boil over medium heat. Boil, covered, for 3½ minutes. 3. Meanwhile, place a fine-mesh strainer over a bowl. 4. Pour the hot cauliflower into the strainer, allowing the bowl to catch the boiling water. With a spoon, press down on the cauliflower to remove as much water as possible. 5. Discard the cooking water and place the cauliflower in the bowl, then add the eggs, almond flour, nutritional yeast, chives, salt, and spices. Stir until everything is incorporated. 6. Heat a large frying pan over medium-low heat. Add the oil and allow to melt completely. 7. Using a ¼-cup (60-ml) scoop, scoop up a portion of the mixture and roll between your hands to form a ball about 1¾ inches (4.5 cm) in diameter. Place in the hot oil and flatten the ball with the back of a fork until it is a patty about ½ inch (1.25 cm) thick. Repeat with the remaining cauliflower mixture, making a total of 10 patties. 8. Cook the patties for 5 minutes per side, or until golden brown. Transfer to a serving plate and enjoy!

Per Serving:
calories: 164 | fat: 12g | protein: 7g | carbs: 7g | net carbs: 3g | fiber: 4g

Chapter **7**

Vegetables and Sides

Butter and Garlic Fried Cabbage

- Oil, for spraying
- ½ head cabbage, cut into bite-size pieces
- 2 tablespoons unsalted butter, melted
- 1 teaspoon granulated garlic
- ½ teaspoon coarse sea salt
- ¼ teaspoon freshly ground black pepper

1. Line the air fryer basket with parchment paper and lightly spray it with oil to prevent sticking. 2. In a large bowl, combine the cabbage, melted butter, minced garlic, salt, and black pepper. Mix well until the cabbage is evenly coated with the ingredients. 3. Transfer the seasoned cabbage to the prepared air fryer basket and spray it lightly with oil again. 4. Air fry at 375°F (191°C) for 5 minutes. After 5 minutes, toss the cabbage to ensure even cooking, then continue to air fry for an additional 3 to 4 minutes, or until the cabbage is lightly crispy. Enjoy your delicious air-fried cabbage!

Per Serving:
calories: 137| fat: 10g | protein: 3g | carbs: 11g | net carbs: 8g | fiber: 3g

Garlic Brussels Sprouts with Almonds

- 1 pound (454 g) Brussels sprouts
- 1 teaspoon sea salt
- 1 teaspoon garlic powder
- 1 tablespoon butter
- 1 small onion, diced
- 2 cloves garlic, crushed
- 3 strips uncured bacon, cut into ½-inch pieces
- 1 tablespoon extra-fine blanched almond slivers
- ½ cup chicken broth
- 2 tablespoons chopped scallions, for garnish

1. Begin by thoroughly washing the Brussels sprouts and removing any wilted or spoiled leaves. Trim the ends and slice the Brussels sprouts in half vertically. In a large mixing bowl, combine the halved Brussels sprouts, any loose leaves, sea salt, and garlic powder, then mix well. 2. Turn on the Instant Pot by selecting the Sauté function and setting it to More. Insert the inner pot and wait until the display indicates "Hot." 3. Add the butter, onion, and garlic to the pot, sautéing for about 2 minutes or until the onion becomes soft. Next, add the bacon and continue to sauté for 3 minutes, or until the bacon begins to shrivel. If there is excess bacon grease, you can spoon some out at this point; you want enough to flavor

the dish without overwhelming the Brussels sprouts. 4. Push the bacon to one side of the pot and add half of the Brussels sprouts to brown. Place the sprouts flat side down in the inner pot, ensuring they are not overcrowded, and avoid stirring until the sides are nicely browned. 5. Once most of the sides are browned, remove them from the pot and set them aside in a bowl. Add the remaining Brussels sprouts to the inner pot to brown. If necessary, add a bit more bacon grease to prevent burning. After they are browned, return the first batch of Brussels sprouts to the pot, then add the almonds and chicken broth. Mix everything together while scraping the bottom of the pot to release any flavorful bits. 6. Press Cancel, then select the Manual button and set the timer for 8 minutes on High Pressure. 7. Secure the lid tightly and adjust the steam release handle to the Sealing position. When the timer goes off, carefully turn the steam release handle to the Venting position to allow steam to escape and the float valve to drop. Press Cancel and open the lid. 8. Finally, garnish with chopped scallions and serve immediately.

Per Serving:
calories: 128 | fat: 6g | protein: 7g | carbs: 15g | net carbs: 10g | fiber: 5g

Mushroom Stroganoff with Vodka

- 2 tablespoons olive oil
- ½ teaspoon crushed caraway seeds
- ½ cup chopped onion
- 2 garlic cloves, smashed
- ¼ cup vodka
- ¾ pound (340 g) button
- mushrooms, chopped
- 1 celery stalk, chopped
- 1 ripe tomato, puréed
- 1 teaspoon mustard seeds
- Sea salt and freshly ground pepper, to taste
- 2 cups vegetable broth

1. Press the Sauté button on your Instant Pot to heat it up. Once hot, add the oil and sauté the caraway seeds until fragrant, about 40 seconds. 2. Next, add the chopped onion and minced garlic, continuing to sauté for an additional 1 to 2 minutes, stirring frequently until the onion is translucent. 3. After that, add the remaining ingredients to the pot and stir to combine everything well. 4. Secure the lid on the Instant Pot. Select Manual mode and set it to High Pressure; cook for 5 minutes. Once the cooking time is complete, perform a quick pressure release and carefully remove the lid. 5. Ladle the contents into individual bowls and serve warm. Bon appétit!

Per Serving:
calories: 128 | fat: 9g | protein: 6g | carbs: 7g | net carbs: 4g | fiber: 3g

Spicy Citrus Slaw

- 1 tablespoon extra-virgin olive oil
- Grated zest of 1 lemon
- Grated zest of 1 lime
- 1 tablespoon lemon juice
- 1 tablespoon lime juice
- A few pinches of sea salt
- 1 (16-ounce / 454-g) bag coleslaw mix (or about ½ head of cabbage and 1 carrot, shredded)
- 1 jalapeño pepper, sliced, seeded if desired for less heat (optional)

1. In a large mixing bowl, combine the olive oil, lemon zest, lime zest, lemon juice, lime juice, and salt. Whisk the mixture until it is well combined and emulsified. 2. Add the slaw mix to the bowl, along with the chopped jalapeño (if using). Toss everything together until the slaw mix is evenly coated with the dressing and the ingredients are well distributed. 3. Let the slaw sit for a few minutes to allow the flavors to meld before serving. Enjoy your refreshing slaw!

Per Serving:
calories: 82 | fat: 4g | protein: 2g | carbs: 13g | net carbs: 8g | fiber: 5g

Asparagus and Mushroom Soup

- 2 tablespoons coconut oil
- ½ cup chopped shallots
- 2 cloves garlic, minced
- 1 pound (454 g) asparagus, washed, trimmed, and chopped
- 4 ounces (113 g) button mushrooms, sliced
- 4 cups vegetable broth
- 2 tablespoons balsamic vinegar
- Himalayan salt, to taste
- ¼ teaspoon ground black pepper
- ¼ teaspoon paprika
- ¼ cup vegan sour cream

1. Start by pressing the Sauté button on your Instant Pot to heat it up. Add the oil and cook the chopped shallots and minced garlic for 2 to 3 minutes, stirring frequently, until they are fragrant and the shallots are translucent. 2. Next, add the remaining ingredients (except for the sour cream) to the Instant Pot. Stir well to combine everything. 3. Secure the lid on the Instant Pot. Select Manual mode and set it to High Pressure; cook for 4 minutes. Once the cooking time is complete, perform a quick pressure release by carefully turning the valve to release the steam. Once the pressure has fully released, carefully remove the lid. 4. Spoon the soup into four bowls. Add a dollop of sour cream to each serving for added creaminess and flavor. Serve immediately and enjoy your delicious soup! Bon appétit!

Per Serving:
calories: 171 | fat: 12g | protein: 10g | carbs: 9g | net carbs: 6g | fiber: 3g

Lemon Broccoli

- 2 cups broccoli florets
- 1 tablespoon ground paprika
- 1 tablespoon lemon juice
- 1 teaspoon grated lemon
- zest
- 1 teaspoon olive oil
- ½ teaspoon chili powder
- 1 cup water

1. Pour the water into the Instant Pot and insert the trivet. 2. In a separate bowl, stir together the remaining ingredients until well combined. 3. Place the pan with the mixture on top of the trivet in the Instant Pot. 4. Set the lid in place, ensuring it is sealed. Select the Manual mode and set the cooking time for 4 minutes on High Pressure. When the timer goes off, perform a quick pressure release. Carefully open the lid. 5. Serve the dish immediately and enjoy!

Per Serving:
calories: 34 | fat: 2g | protein: 2g | carbs: 4g | net carbs: 2g | fiber: 2g

Zoodles and Doodles

For Zoodles:
- 2 medium zucchinis (about 7 ounces/200 g each), green or yellow

For Doodles:
- 1 medium daikon (about 14 ounces/400 g)

1. If you have a spiralizer, follow the manufacturer's instructions to slice a zucchini or daikon into noodles. If you're using a vegetable peeler, hold the zucchini or daikon in your non-dominant hand over a bowl. With your other hand, start peeling the vegetable. The length of the ribbons will depend on how far down you peel; for shorter ribbons, simply peel a smaller section. Continue this process until most of the zucchini or daikon has been transformed into ribbons, leaving just a small, long core in your hand. 2. If you want to make Zoodles, repeat the same process with a second zucchini. 3. You can use the noodles right away in your dish or store them as instructed. Enjoy your fresh vegetable noodles!

Per Serving:
calories: 16 | fat: 0g | protein: 1g | carbs: 3g | net carbs: 2g | fiber: 1g

Cauliflower Curry

- 1 pound (454 g) cauliflower, chopped
- 3 ounces (85 g) scallions, chopped
- 1 cup coconut milk
- ¼ cup crushed tomatoes
- 1 tablespoon coconut oil
- 1 teaspoon garam masala
- 1 teaspoon ground turmeric

1. Add all the ingredients to the Instant Pot and stir to combine thoroughly. 2. Lock the lid in place. Select the Manual mode and set the cooking time for 3 minutes at High Pressure. When the timer goes off, allow for a natural pressure release for 5 minutes, then release any remaining pressure. Carefully open the lid. 3. Stir the cooked dish well to ensure everything is evenly mixed before serving. Enjoy your meal!

Per Serving:

calories: 142 | fat: 12g | protein: 3g | carbs: 8g | net carbs: 5g | fiber: 4g

Bacon-y Caramelized Onions

- 2 tablespoons bacon fat
- 4 small yellow onions, thinly sliced
- ½ teaspoon sea salt
- ½ teaspoon dried rosemary leaves or thyme leaves (optional)

1. Begin by heating a large sauté pan or skillet over medium heat and melting the bacon fat. Once the fat is fully melted, add the sliced onions to the pan. Sauté the onions for about 8 to 10 minutes, or until they start to become translucent. At this point, sprinkle in the salt and, if desired, the dried rosemary to enhance the flavor. 2. After the onions have softened, reduce the heat to medium-low. Continue to cook the onions slowly for approximately 45 minutes, stirring occasionally. Allow the onions to develop a slight browning before each stir. If you notice that the onions are browning too quickly or beginning to stick to the bottom of the pan, lower the heat further. You can also add 1 to 2 tablespoons of warm water as needed, stirring it in to help keep the onions cooking evenly without burning. 3. Throughout the cooking process, the onions will gradually become more caramelized, deepening in color and flavor. They should eventually reach a beautifully rich and golden-brown appearance, similar to what you see in the accompanying photo. This method requires patience and low, slow heat; attempting to rush the process with higher temperatures will not yield the same deliciously rich results. Enjoy the transformation of the onions as

they become a flavorful addition to your dish!

Per Serving:

calories: 85 | fat: 6g | protein: 1g | carbs: 7g | net carbs: 6g | fiber: 1g

Easy Cheesy Caulirice

- 2 tablespoons salted butter
- 1 (12-ounce) bag frozen riced cauliflower
- ½ cup shredded cheddar cheese
- 2 tablespoons heavy whipping cream
- Salt and ground black pepper

1. Begin by melting the butter in a medium-sized skillet over medium heat. 2. Once the butter is melted, add the cauliflower to the skillet and cook, stirring occasionally, until it becomes tender, which should take about 15 minutes. 3. After the cauliflower is tender, turn off the heat and add the cheese and cream to the skillet. Stir the mixture until the cheese is completely melted and all the ingredients are well combined. 4. Finally, season the dish to taste with salt and pepper, and serve immediately for the best flavor and texture.

Per Serving:

calories: 156 | fat: 14g | protein: 5g | carbs: 5g | net carbs: 3g | fiber: 2g

Cheesy Mashed Cauliflower

- 1 head cauliflower, chopped roughly
- ½ cup shredded Cheddar cheese
- ¼ cup heavy (whipping)
- cream
- 2 tablespoons butter, at room temperature
- Sea salt
- Freshly ground black pepper

1. Fill a large saucepan three-quarters full with water and place it over high heat to bring it to a boil. 2. Blanch the cauliflower in the boiling water until it becomes tender, which should take about 5 minutes, then drain it. 3. Transfer the drained cauliflower to a food processor, adding the cheese, heavy cream, and butter. Purée the mixture until it is very creamy and whipped. 4. Season the purée with salt and pepper to taste. 5. Serve immediately.

Per Serving:

calories: 183 | fat: 15g | protein: 8g | carbs: 6g | net carbs: 4g | fiber: 2g

Savory and Rich Creamed Kale

Prep time: 10 minutes | Cook time: 5 minutes | Serves 4

- 2 tablespoons extra-virgin olive oil
- 2 cloves garlic, crushed
- 1 small onion, chopped
- 12 ounces (340 g) kale, finely chopped
- ½ cup chicken broth
- 1 teaspoon Herbes de Provence
- 4 ounces (113 g) cream cheese
- ½ cup full-fat heavy cream
- 1 teaspoon dried tarragon

1. Start by pressing the Sauté button on the Instant Pot and allowing the olive oil to heat up. Once hot, add the minced garlic and chopped onion to the pot, sautéing for about 2 minutes or until the onion becomes soft and translucent. Next, incorporate the kale, chicken broth, and Herbes de Provence into the mixture. 2. After adding the ingredients, lock the lid securely in place. Select the Manual mode and set the cooking time to 3 minutes at High Pressure. Once the timer goes off, perform a quick pressure release to release the steam. Carefully open the lid to avoid any hot steam. 3. Finally, stir in the cream cheese, heavy cream, and tarragon, mixing thoroughly to ensure the dish thickens nicely. Serve the dish immediately for the best flavor and texture.

Per Serving:

calories: 229 | fat: 19g | protein: 6g | carbs: 12g | net carbs: 9g | fiber: 3g

Sautéed Cabbage with Bacon

Prep time: 10 minutes | Cook time: 15 minutes | Serves 4

- 1 medium head of green cabbage
- 6 slices bacon (no sugar added)
- 1 large leek, white part sliced
- ½ cup chopped onion
- 3 garlic cloves, minced
- 2 teaspoons kosher salt
- 1 teaspoon black pepper
- ½ teaspoon sweet paprika

1. Begin by using a very sharp knife to cut the cabbage into quarters, then remove and discard the core. Next, chop the cabbage into thin strips. 2. Take kitchen shears and cut the bacon into small pieces for easier cooking. 3. Heat a large skillet over medium-high heat and add the bacon. Cook the bacon until it starts to become crispy. Then, add the chopped leek and onion to the skillet. Stir frequently and cook until the vegetables are nicely browned, which should take about 3 minutes. After that, add the minced garlic and cook for an additional minute. 4. Now, stir in the chopped cabbage along with salt, pepper, and paprika. Continue to stir and cook

for about 10 minutes. You can serve the dish at this point, or for a different texture, reduce the heat to low, cover the skillet, and let it cook for an additional 30 minutes, stirring occasionally. This longer cooking time will yield much softer cabbage with a richer bacon flavor.

Per Serving:

calories: 262 | fat: 16g | protein: 10g | carbs: 20g | net carbs: 11g | fiber: 9g

Marinated Onions

Prep time: 10 minutes | Cook time: 0 minutes | Makes about 2 cups

- ⅓ cup red wine vinegar
- 1 teaspoon coarse or flake sea salt, or ½ teaspoon fine sea salt
- 1 teaspoon dried oregano leaves or dried chives
- ½ teaspoon garlic powder
- ¼ teaspoon ground black pepper
- 2 medium red onions, cut in ¼-inch-thick half moons

1. In a medium-sized mixing bowl, combine the oil, vinegar, salt, and spices. Add the onions and stir to ensure they are well coated. Cover the bowl and let the mixture marinate overnight in the refrigerator. 2. The marinated onions can be stored in an airtight container in the refrigerator for 1 to 2 weeks.

Per Serving:

calories: 26 | fat: 0g | protein: 1g | carbs: 5g | net carbs: 4g | fiber: 1g

Bacon Green Beans

Prep time: 2 minutes | Cook time: 20 minutes | Serves 2

- 2 ounces (57 g) bacon, cut into ½-inch-wide crosswise strips
- 6 ounces (170 g) green
- beans, trimmed
- ½ teaspoon seasoning salt
- ¼ teaspoon red pepper flakes

1. Heat a medium sauté pan or skillet over medium-high heat. Add the bacon and cook for 7 to 10 minutes, stirring occasionally, until the bacon is almost crispy. 2. Reduce the heat to medium-low and add the beans, seasoning salt, and red pepper flakes to the pan. 3. Sauté the beans for 7 to 10 minutes, stirring occasionally, until they are tender but still crisp. 4. Transfer the bacon and beans to a serving plate and enjoy your delicious dish!

Per Serving:

calories: 142 | fat: 11g | protein: 5g | carbs: 6g | net carbs: 4g | fiber: 2g

Broccoli with Sesame Dressing

Prep time: 5 minutes | Cook time: 10 minutes | Serves 4

- 6 cups broccoli florets, cut into bite-size pieces
- 1 tablespoon olive oil
- ¼ teaspoon salt
- 2 tablespoons sesame seeds
- 2 tablespoons rice vinegar
- 2 tablespoons coconut aminos
- 2 tablespoons sesame oil
- ½ teaspoon Swerve
- ¼ teaspoon red pepper flakes (optional)

1. Start by preheating the air fryer to 400ºF (204ºC). 2. In a large bowl, toss the broccoli florets with olive oil and salt until they are thoroughly coated. 3. Next, transfer the seasoned broccoli to the air fryer basket. Air fry for 10 minutes, shaking the basket halfway through the cooking time to ensure even cooking. The broccoli should be tender with crispy edges when done. 4. While the broccoli is cooking, take the same large bowl and whisk together the sesame seeds, vinegar, coconut aminos, sesame oil, Swerve, and red pepper flakes (if using). 5. Once the broccoli is finished cooking, transfer it to the bowl with the dressing and toss until the broccoli is thoroughly coated with the seasonings. Serve warm or at room temperature for the best flavor.

Per Serving:

calories: 133| fat: 13g | protein: 3g | carbs: 3g | net carbs: 1g | fiber: 2g

Faux-tato Salad

Prep time: 20 minutes | Cook time: 10 minutes | Serves 4

- ½ head cauliflower, cut into florets
- ⅓ cup mayonnaise
- 2 tablespoons stone-ground mustard
- 1 tablespoon red wine vinegar
- ¼ teaspoon pink Himalayan sea salt
- ¼ teaspoon freshly ground black pepper
- 4 ounces (113 g) bacon, cooked until crisp and chopped
- 1 large egg, hard-boiled, peeled, and chopped
- ¼ medium red onion, thinly sliced
- 2 tablespoons grated Cheddar cheese
- 2 scallions, white and green parts, chopped

1. Set a steamer basket in a small pot and add a couple of inches of

water. Place the cauliflower florets in the steamer basket, cover the pot, and steam for 7 to 10 minutes, or until the cauliflower is tender but not mushy. Once done, remove from heat and let it cool. 2. In a small bowl, combine the mayonnaise, mustard, vinegar, salt, and pepper. Mix well to create the dressing. 3. In a large bowl, combine the cooled cauliflower, cooked bacon, chopped hard-boiled eggs, red onion, cheese, and scallions. 4. Pour the dressing over the salad and mix everything together until well combined. If desired, place the bowl in the refrigerator to chill the salad for about 1 hour before serving. Enjoy your delicious cauliflower salad!

Per Serving:

calories: 287 | fat: 27g | protein: 7g | carbs: 3g | net carbs: 2g | fiber: 1g

Roasted Radishes with Brown Butter Sauce

Prep time: 10 minutes | Cook time: 15 minutes | Serves 2

- 2 cups halved radishes
- 1 tablespoon olive oil
- Pink Himalayan salt
- Freshly ground black pepper
- 2 tablespoons butter
- 1 tablespoon chopped fresh flat-leaf Italian parsley

1. Preheat your oven to 450°F (232°C). 2. In a medium bowl, toss the radishes with olive oil, ensuring they are well coated. Season with pink Himalayan salt and pepper to taste. 3. Spread the seasoned radishes on a baking sheet in a single layer. Roast in the preheated oven for 15 minutes, stirring halfway through to ensure even cooking. 4. While the radishes are roasting, prepare the browned butter. In a small, light-colored saucepan over medium heat, melt the butter completely, stirring frequently. Season the butter with a pinch of pink Himalayan salt. As the butter begins to bubble and foam, continue stirring. When the bubbling diminishes and the butter turns a nice nutty brown, which should take about 3 minutes, remove it from the heat and transfer the browned butter to a heat-safe container (like a mug). 5. Once the radishes are done roasting, remove them from the oven and divide them between two plates. Spoon the browned butter over the radishes, sprinkle with chopped parsley, and serve immediately. Enjoy your delicious roasted radishes!

Per Serving:

calories: 181 | fat: 19g | protein: 1g | carbs: 4g | net carbs: 2g | fiber: 2g

Chinese-Style Pe-Tsai with Onion

Prep time: 5 minutes | Cook time: 8 minutes | Serves 4

- 2 tablespoons sesame oil
- 1 yellow onion, chopped
- 1 pound (454 g) pe-tsai cabbage, shredded
- ¼ cup rice wine vinegar
- 1 tablespoon coconut

- aminos
- 1 teaspoon finely minced garlic
- ½ teaspoon salt
- ¼ teaspoon Szechuan pepper

1. Begin by setting the Instant Pot to the Sauté mode and heating the sesame oil. Once hot, add the chopped onion to the pot and sauté for about 5 minutes, or until the onion is tender. Then, stir in the remaining ingredients. 2. After mixing in the ingredients, lock the lid of the Instant Pot. Select the Manual mode and set the cooking time for 3 minutes on High Pressure. When the timer goes off, perform a quick pressure release by carefully turning the valve to release the steam. Once the pressure has been released, carefully open the lid. 3. Finally, transfer the cabbage mixture to a bowl and serve immediately for the best flavor and texture. Enjoy!

Per Serving:

calories: 96 | fat: 7g | protein: 2g | carbs: 7g | net carbs: 5 g | fiber: 2g

Cheesy Zucchini Gratin

Prep time: 10 minutes | Cook time: 40 minutes | Serves 6

- 4 tablespoons butter
- 1 large onion, sliced
- 2 garlic cloves, minced
- 1 cup heavy (whipping) cream
- ¼ cup cream cheese

- Salt, to taste
- Freshly ground black pepper, to taste
- 4 or 5 large zucchini, cut into ¼-inch-thick rounds
- ¾ cup shredded white Cheddar cheese

1. In a large saucepan over medium-low heat, melt the butter until it is fully melted and bubbling. 2. Add the chopped onion and minced garlic to the saucepan. Cook for about 15 minutes, stirring occasionally, until the garlic is fragrant and the onion begins to caramelize. Once the onions are caramelized, reduce the heat to low. 3. Stir in the cream and let it simmer for 2 minutes, allowing the flavors to meld. 4. Next, add the cream cheese to the saucepan. Season the mixture with salt and pepper, and stir until the sauce is smooth and creamy. 5. Place the sliced zucchini in a 7-by-11-inch baking dish and pour the cream sauce over the top, ensuring the zucchini is well coated. Sprinkle the Cheddar cheese on top and bake in a preheated oven for about 20 minutes, or until the cheese is melted and turns golden brown. Allow the dish to cool slightly before serving. Store any leftovers in an airtight container in the refrigerator for up to 4 days. Enjoy!

Per Serving:

calories: 307 | fat: 30g | protein: 6g | carbs: 5g | net carbs: 4g | fiber: 1g

Old-School Buttered (Zucchini) Noodles

Prep time: 20 minutes | Cook time: 10 minutes | Serves 2

- 2 medium zucchini, spiralized or peeled into thin strips
- Salt, to taste
- 3 tablespoons butter
- 1 garlic clove, minced

- ¼ cup grated Parmesan cheese
- Freshly ground black pepper, to taste
- Fresh parsley leaves, chopped, for garnish

1. Start by placing the zucchini noodles in a colander and sprinkling them liberally with salt. Allow them to sit in the sink for 15 to 20 minutes. This process helps draw out excess moisture. After the time has passed, rinse the noodles under cold water and pat them dry with a paper towel to remove any excess salt and moisture. 2. In a large skillet over medium-low heat, melt the butter until it is fully melted and bubbling. 3. Add the minced garlic to the skillet and sauté for 3 to 4 minutes, stirring frequently, until the garlic is fragrant and lightly golden. 4. Next, add the zucchini noodles to the skillet, tossing to combine with the garlic and butter. Cook for 5 to 6 minutes, or until the noodles are softened but still have a slight bite. Season with salt and pepper to taste. 5. Remove the skillet from the heat and top the zucchini noodles with freshly grated Parmesan cheese and some chopped parsley for garnish. Serve immediately and enjoy!

Per Serving:

calories: 209 | fat: 21g | protein: 5g | carbs: 2g | net carbs: 2g | fiber: 0g

Stir Fried Asparagus and Kale

Prep time: 5 minutes | Cook time: 3 minutes | Serves 4

- 8 ounces (227 g) asparagus, chopped
- 2 cups chopped kale
- 2 bell peppers, chopped
- 1 tablespoon avocado oil
- 1 teaspoon apple cider vinegar
- ½ teaspoon minced ginger
- ½ cup water

1. Pour the water into the Instant Pot. 2. In the Instant Pot pan, stir together the remaining ingredients until well combined. 3. Insert the trivet into the Instant Pot and place the pan with the mixture on top of the trivet. 4. Set the lid in place, ensuring it is sealed properly. Select the Manual mode and set the cooking time for 3 minutes on High Pressure. Once the timer goes off, perform a quick pressure release by carefully turning the valve to release the steam. 5. After the pressure has been released, carefully open the lid. Serve the dish immediately and enjoy!

Per Serving:

calories: 56 | fat: 4g | protein: 2g | carbs: 4g | net carbs: 2g | fiber: 2g

Zucchini and Daikon Fritters

Prep time: 10 minutes | Cook time: 8 minutes | Serves 4

- 2 large zucchinis, grated
- 1 daikon, diced
- 1 egg, beaten
- 1 teaspoon ground flax meal
- 1 teaspoon salt
- 1 tablespoon coconut oil

1. In a mixing bowl, combine all the ingredients for the fritters, except for the coconut oil. Mix well until everything is evenly incorporated. Once combined, form the mixture into small fritters, shaping them to your desired size. 2. Press the Sauté button on the Instant Pot and add the coconut oil. Allow the oil to melt and heat up until it shimmers. 3. Carefully place the zucchini fritters in the hot oil, making sure not to overcrowd the pot. Cook for about 4 minutes on each side, or until they are golden brown and crispy. 4. Once cooked, transfer the fritters to a plate lined with paper towels to absorb any excess oil. Serve warm and enjoy your delicious zucchini fritters!

Per Serving:

calories: 77 | fat: 5g | protein: 4g | carbs: 6g | net carbs: 4g | fiber: 2g

Green Bean Bacon Bundles

Prep time: 15 minutes | Cook time: 25 minutes | serves 4

- 12 ounces fresh green beans (about 2 cups), trimmed
- 2 tablespoons avocado oil
- 8 slices bacon, cut in half crosswise
- ½ teaspoon salt
- ¼ teaspoon ground black pepper

1. Preheat your oven to 400°F (200°C) and line a sheet pan with parchment paper to prevent sticking. 2. In a mixing bowl, toss the green beans with the oil until they are evenly coated. 3. Take a few green beans (about 4 or 5, depending on their size and the length of the bacon) and wrap them with a slice of bacon, securing the bundle. Place each bundle on the prepared sheet pan with the seam of the bacon facing down to hold it in place. Once all the bundles are arranged, sprinkle them evenly with salt and pepper. 4. Bake in the preheated oven for 25 minutes, or until the bacon is crispy and the green beans are tender. Keep an eye on them towards the end to ensure they reach your desired level of crispness. Enjoy your delicious bacon-wrapped green beans!

Per Serving:

calories: 186 | fat: 16g | protein: 8g | carbs: 4g | net carbs: 2g | fiber: 1g

Tomato and Artichoke Mushroom Pizzas

Prep time: 10 minutes | Cook time: 20 minutes | Serves 2

- 2 large portobello mushroom caps
- ¼ cup tomato sauce
- ½ teaspoon Italian seasoning
- ¼ teaspoon pink Himalayan sea salt
- ½ cup shredded low-moisture mozzarella cheese
- 2 tablespoons chopped canned artichoke hearts
- ¼ cup halved cherry tomatoes

1. Preheat your oven to 350°F (180°C) and line a baking sheet with aluminum foil for easy cleanup. 2. Place the mushroom caps upside down on the prepared baking sheet. 3. In a small bowl, combine the tomato sauce, Italian seasoning, and salt. Divide the sauce evenly between the two mushroom caps, spreading it inside each cap. 4. Add 2 tablespoons of mozzarella cheese to each mushroom cap, distributing it evenly. 5. Top the cheese with artichoke hearts and halved cherry tomatoes. Then, sprinkle the remaining ¼ cup of mozzarella cheese over the tops of the stuffed mushrooms. 6. Bake in the preheated oven for 20 minutes, or until the cheese is melted and bubbly. Remove from the oven and serve warm. Enjoy your delicious stuffed mushrooms!

Per Serving:

calories: 121 | fat: 6g | protein: 10g | carbs: 9g | net carbs: 6g | fiber: 3g

Cauliflower "Potato" Salad

Prep time: 10 minutes | Cook time: 25 minutes | Serves 2

- ½ head cauliflower
- 1 tablespoon olive oil
- Pink Himalayan salt
- Freshly ground black pepper
- ⅓ cup mayonnaise
- 1 tablespoon mustard
- ¼ cup diced dill pickles
- 1 teaspoon paprika

1. Preheat your oven to 400°F (200°C) and line a baking sheet with aluminum foil or a silicone baking mat for easy cleanup. 2. Cut the cauliflower into 1-inch pieces and place them in a large bowl. 3. Add the olive oil to the bowl, then season the cauliflower with pink Himalayan salt and pepper. Toss everything together until the cauliflower is evenly coated. 4. Spread the seasoned cauliflower out on the prepared baking sheet in a single layer. Bake in the preheated oven for 25 minutes, or until the cauliflower begins to brown. Halfway through the cooking time, give the pan a couple of shakes or stir the cauliflower to ensure even cooking. 5. Once the cauliflower is done roasting, remove it from the oven and let it cool slightly. In a large bowl, mix the roasted cauliflower with mayonnaise, mustard, and pickles until well combined. Sprinkle paprika on top for added flavor and color. Chill the mixture in the refrigerator for at least 3 hours before serving to allow the flavors to meld. Enjoy your delicious cauliflower salad!

Per Serving:

calories: 386 | fat: 37g | protein: 5g | carbs: 13g | net carbs: 8g | fiber: 5g

Chapter **8**

Vegetarian Mains

Cheesy Crustless Vegetable Quiche

Prep time: 5 minutes | Cook time: 25 minutes | Serves 4

- 1 tablespoon grass-fed butter, divided
- 6 eggs
- ¾ cup heavy (whipping) cream
- 3 ounces goat cheese, divided
- ½ cup sliced mushrooms, chopped
- 1 scallion, white and green parts, chopped
- 1 cup shredded fresh spinach
- 10 cherry tomatoes, cut in half

1. Preheat the oven. Set the oven temperature to 350°F. Grease a 9-inch pie plate with ½ teaspoon of the butter and set it aside. 2. Mix the quiche base. In a medium bowl, whisk the eggs, cream, and 2 ounces of the cheese until it's all well blended. Set it aside. 3. Sauté the vegetables. In a small skillet over medium-high heat, melt the remaining butter. Add the mushrooms and scallion and sauté them until they've softened, about 2 minutes. Add the spinach and sauté until it's wilted, about 2 minutes. 4. Assemble and bake. Spread the vegetable mixture in the bottom of the pie plate and pour the egg-and-cream mixture over the vegetables. Scatter the cherry tomatoes and the remaining 1 ounce of goat cheese on top. Bake for 20 to 25 minutes until the quiche is cooked through, puffed, and lightly browned. 5. Serve. Cut the quiche into wedges and divide it between four plates. Serve it warm or cold.

Per Serving:
calories: 355 | fat: 30g | protein: 18g | carbs: 5g | net carbs: 4g | fiber: 1g

Buttery Almond-Cauliflower Gnocchi

Prep time: 5 minutes | Cook time: 25 to 30 minutes | Serves 4

- 5 cups cauliflower florets
- ⅔ cup almond flour
- ½ teaspoon salt
- ¼ cup unsalted butter, melted
- ¼ cup grated Parmesan cheese

1. In a food processor fitted with a metal blade, pulse the cauliflower until finely chopped. Transfer the cauliflower to a large microwave-safe bowl and cover it with a paper towel. Microwave for 5 minutes. Spread the cauliflower on a towel to cool. 2. When cool enough to handle, draw up the sides of the towel and squeeze tightly over a sink to remove the excess moisture. Return the cauliflower to the food processor and whirl until creamy. Sprinkle in the flour and salt and pulse until a sticky dough comes together. 3. Transfer the dough to a workspace lightly floured with almond flour. Shape the dough into a ball and divide into 4 equal sections. Roll each section into a rope 1 inch thick. Slice the dough into squares with a sharp knife. 4. Preheat the air fryer to 400°F (204°C). 5. Working in batches if necessary, place the gnocchi in a single layer in the basket of the air fryer and spray generously with olive oil. Pausing halfway through the cooking time to turn the gnocchi, air fry for 25 to 30 minutes until golden brown and crispy on the edges. Transfer to a large bowl and toss with the melted butter and Parmesan cheese.

Per Serving:
calories: 220 | fat: 20g | protein: 7g | carbs: 8g | net carbs: 5g | fiber: 3g

Stuffed Mushrooms with Spinach and Artichokes

Prep time: 10 minutes | Cook time: 10 to 14 minutes | Serves 4

- 2 tablespoons olive oil
- 4 large portobello mushrooms, stems removed and gills scraped out
- ½ teaspoon salt
- ¼ teaspoon freshly ground pepper
- 4 ounces (113 g) goat cheese, crumbled
- ½ cup chopped marinated artichoke hearts
- 1 cup frozen spinach, thawed and squeezed dry
- ½ cup grated Parmesan cheese
- 2 tablespoons chopped fresh parsley

1. Preheat the air fryer to 400°F (204°C). 2. Rub the olive oil over the portobello mushrooms until thoroughly coated. Sprinkle both sides with the salt and black pepper. Place top-side down on a clean work surface. 3. In a small bowl, combine the goat cheese, artichoke hearts, and spinach. Mash with the back of a fork until thoroughly combined. Divide the cheese mixture among the mushrooms and sprinkle with the Parmesan cheese. 4. Air fry for 10 to 14 minutes until the mushrooms are tender and the cheese has begun to brown. Top with the fresh parsley just before serving.

Per Serving:
calories: 255 | fat: 20g | protein: 13g | carbs: 7g | net carbs: 4g | fiber: 3g

Classic Eggplant Parmesan

Prep time: 15 minutes | Cook time: 17 minutes | Serves 4

- 1 medium eggplant, ends trimmed, sliced into ½-inch rounds
- ¼ teaspoon salt
- 2 tablespoons coconut oil
- ½ cup grated Parmesan cheese
- 1 ounce (28 g) 100% cheese crisps, finely crushed
- ½ cup low-carb marinara sauce
- ½ cup shredded Mozzarella cheese

1. Sprinkle eggplant rounds with salt on both sides and wrap in a kitchen towel for 30 minutes. Press to remove excess water, then drizzle rounds with coconut oil on both sides. 2. In a medium bowl, mix Parmesan and cheese crisps. Press each eggplant slice into mixture to coat both sides. 3. Place rounds into ungreased air fryer basket. Adjust the temperature to 350ºF (177ºC) and air fry for 15 minutes, turning rounds halfway through cooking. They will be crispy around the edges when done. 4. Spoon marinara over rounds and sprinkle with Mozzarella. Continue cooking an additional 2 minutes at 350ºF (177ºC) until cheese is melted. Serve warm.

Per Serving:

calories: 208 | fat: 13g | protein: 12g | carbs: 13g | net carbs: 8g | fiber: 5g

Roasted Lemon-Infused Cauliflower

Prep time: 5 minutes | Cook time: 15 minutes | Serves 4

- 1 medium head cauliflower
- 2 tablespoons salted butter, melted
- 1 medium lemon
- ½ teaspoon garlic powder
- 1 teaspoon dried parsley

1. Remove the leaves from the head of cauliflower and brush it with melted butter. Cut the lemon in half and zest one half onto the cauliflower. Squeeze the juice of the zested lemon half and pour it over the cauliflower. 2. Sprinkle with garlic powder and parsley. Place cauliflower head into the air fryer basket. 3. Adjust the temperature to 350ºF (177ºC) and air fry for 15 minutes. 4. Check cauliflower every 5 minutes to avoid overcooking. It should be fork tender. 5. To serve, squeeze juice from other lemon half over cauliflower. Serve immediately.

Per Serving:

calories: 90 | fat: 7g | protein: 3g | carbs: 6g | net carbs: 4g | fiber: 2g

Spinach Pesto Flatbread

Prep time: 10 minutes | Cook time: 8 minutes | Serves 4

- 1 cup blanched finely ground almond flour
- 2 ounces (57 g) cream cheese
- 2 cups shredded Mozzarella
- cheese
- 1 cup chopped fresh spinach leaves
- 2 tablespoons basil pesto

1. Place flour, cream cheese, and Mozzarella in a large microwave-safe bowl and microwave on high 45 seconds, then stir. 2. Fold in spinach and microwave an additional 15 seconds. Stir until a soft dough ball forms. 3. Cut two pieces of parchment paper to fit air fryer basket. Separate dough into two sections and press each out on ungreased parchment to create 6-inch rounds. 4. Spread 1 tablespoon pesto over each flatbread and place rounds on parchment into ungreased air fryer basket. Adjust the temperature to 350ºF (177ºC) and air fry for 8 minutes, turning crusts halfway through cooking. Flatbread will be golden when done. 5. Let cool 5 minutes before slicing and serving.

Per Serving:

calories: 387 | fat: 28g | protein: 28g | carbs: 10g | net carbs: 5g | fiber: 5g

Zucchini Boats with Cheese Filling

Prep time: 20 minutes | Cook time: 8 minutes | Serves 4

- 1 large zucchini, cut into four pieces
- 2 tablespoons olive oil
- 1 cup Ricotta cheese, room temperature
- 2 tablespoons scallions, chopped
- 1 heaping tablespoon fresh parsley, roughly chopped
- 1 heaping tablespoon coriander, minced
- 2 ounces (57 g) Cheddar cheese, preferably freshly grated
- 1 teaspoon celery seeds
- ½ teaspoon salt
- ½ teaspoon garlic pepper

1. Cook your zucchini in the air fryer basket for approximately 10 minutes at 350ºF (177ºC). Check for doneness and cook for 2-3 minutes longer if needed. 2. Meanwhile, make the stuffing by mixing the other items. 3. When your zucchini is thoroughly cooked, open them up. Divide the stuffing among all zucchini pieces and bake an additional 5 minutes.

Per Serving:

calories: 242 | fat: 20g | protein: 12g | carbs: 5g | net carbs: 4g | fiber: 1g

Cheesy Broccoli Crust Pizza

Prep time: 15 minutes | Cook time: 12 minutes | Serves 4

- 3 cups riced broccoli, steamed and drained well
- 1 large egg
- ½ cup grated vegetarian Parmesan cheese
- 3 tablespoons low-carb Alfredo sauce
- ½ cup shredded Mozzarella cheese

1. In a large bowl, mix broccoli, egg, and Parmesan. 2. Cut a piece of parchment to fit your air fryer basket. Press out the pizza mixture to fit on the parchment, working in two batches if necessary. Place into the air fryer basket. 3. Adjust the temperature to 370ºF (188ºC) and air fry for 5 minutes. 4. The crust should be firm enough to flip. If not, add 2 additional minutes. Flip crust. 5. Top with Alfredo sauce and Mozzarella. Return to the air fryer basket and cook an additional 7 minutes or until cheese is golden and bubbling. Serve warm.

Per Serving:
calories: 178 | fat: 11g | protein: 15g | carbs: 10g | net carbs: 4g | fiber: 6g

Crunchy Fried Tofu

Prep time: 30 minutes | Cook time: 15 to 20 minutes | Serves 4

- 1 (16-ounce / 454-g) block extra-firm tofu
- 2 tablespoons coconut aminos
- 1 tablespoon toasted sesame oil
- 1 tablespoon olive oil
- 1 tablespoon chili-garlic sauce
- 1½ teaspoons black sesame seeds
- 1 scallion, thinly sliced

1. Press the tofu for at least 15 minutes by wrapping it in paper towels and setting a heavy pan on top so that the moisture drains. 2. Slice the tofu into bite-size cubes and transfer to a bowl. Drizzle with the coconut aminos, sesame oil, olive oil, and chili-garlic sauce. Cover and refrigerate for 1 hour or up to overnight. 3. Preheat the air fryer to 400ºF (204ºC). 4. Arrange the tofu in a single layer in the air fryer basket. Pausing to shake the pan halfway through the cooking time, air fry for 15 to 20 minutes until crisp. Serve with any juices that accumulate in the bottom of the air fryer, sprinkled with the sesame seeds and sliced scallion.

Per Serving:
calories: 186 | fat: 14g | protein: 12g | carbs: 4g | net carbs: 3g | fiber: 1g

Mediterranean-Style Pan Pizza

Prep time: 5 minutes | Cook time: 8 minutes | Serves 2

- 1 cup shredded Mozzarella cheese
- ¼ medium red bell pepper, seeded and chopped
- ½ cup chopped fresh
- spinach leaves
- 2 tablespoons chopped black olives
- 2 tablespoons crumbled feta cheese

1. Sprinkle Mozzarella into an ungreased round nonstick baking dish in an even layer. Add remaining ingredients on top. 2. Place dish into air fryer basket. Adjust the temperature to 350ºF (177ºC) and bake for 8 minutes, checking halfway through to avoid burning. Top of pizza will be golden brown and the cheese melted when done. 3. Remove dish from fryer and let cool 5 minutes before slicing and serving.

Per Serving:
calories: 239 | fat: 17g | protein: 17g | carbs: 6g | net carbs: 5g | fiber: 1g

Ricotta-Stuffed Mushrooms with Herbs

Prep time: 10 minutes | Cook time: 30 minutes | Serves 4

- 6 tablespoons extra-virgin olive oil, divided
- 4 portobello mushroom caps, cleaned and gills removed
- 1 cup whole-milk ricotta cheese
- ⅓ cup chopped fresh herbs
- (such as basil, parsley, rosemary, oregano, or thyme)
- 2 garlic cloves, finely minced
- ½ teaspoon salt
- ¼ teaspoon freshly ground black pepper

1. Preheat the oven to 400ºF (205ºC). 2. Line a baking sheet with parchment or foil and drizzle with 2 tablespoons olive oil, spreading evenly. Place the mushroom caps on the baking sheet, gill-side up. 3. In a medium bowl, mix together the ricotta, herbs, 2 tablespoons olive oil, garlic, salt, and pepper. Stuff each mushroom cap with one-quarter of the cheese mixture, pressing down if needed. Drizzle with remaining 2 tablespoons olive oil and bake until golden brown and the mushrooms are soft, 30 to 35 minutes, depending on the size of the mushrooms.

Per Serving:
calories: 308 | fat: 29g | protein: 9g | carbs: 6g | net carbs: 5g | fiber: 1g

Crunchy Eggplant Rounds

Prep time: 15 minutes | Cook time: 10 minutes | Serves 4

- 1 large eggplant, ends trimmed, cut into ½-inch slices
- ½ teaspoon salt
- 2 ounces (57 g) Parmesan

- 100% cheese crisps, finely ground
- ½ teaspoon paprika
- ¼ teaspoon garlic powder
- 1 large egg

1. Sprinkle eggplant rounds with salt. Place rounds on a kitchen towel for 30 minutes to draw out excess water. Pat rounds dry. 2. In a medium bowl, mix cheese crisps, paprika, and garlic powder. In a separate medium bowl, whisk egg. Dip each eggplant round in egg, then gently press into cheese crisps to coat both sides. 3. Place eggplant rounds into ungreased air fryer basket. Adjust the temperature to 400°F (204°C) and air fry for 10 minutes, turning rounds halfway through cooking. Eggplant will be golden and crispy when done. Serve warm.

Per Serving:

calories: 133 | fat: 8g | protein: 10g | carbs: 6g | net carbs: 4g | fiber: 3g

Zucchini Roll Stuffed Manicotti

Prep time: 15 minutes | Cook time: 30 minutes | Serves 4

- Olive oil cooking spray
- 4 zucchini
- 2 tablespoons good-quality olive oil
- 1 red bell pepper, diced
- ½ onion, minced
- 2 teaspoons minced garlic
- 1 cup goat cheese
- 1 cup shredded mozzarella

- cheese
- 1 tablespoon chopped fresh oregano
- Sea salt, for seasoning
- Freshly ground black pepper, for seasoning
- 2 cups low-carb marinara sauce, divided
- ½ cup grated Parmesan cheese

1. Preheat the oven. Set the oven temperature to 375°F. Lightly grease a 9-by-13-inch baking dish with olive oil cooking spray. 2. Prepare the zucchini. Cut the zucchini lengthwise into ⅛-inch-thick slices and set them aside. 3. Make the filling. In a medium skillet over medium-high heat, warm the olive oil. Add the red bell pepper, onion, and garlic and sauté until they've softened, about 4 minutes. Remove the skillet from the heat and transfer the vegetables to a medium bowl. Stir the goat cheese, mozzarella, and oregano into the vegetables. Season it all with salt and pepper. 4. Assemble the manicotti. Spread 1 cup of the marinara sauce in the bottom of the baking dish. Lay a zucchini slice on a clean cutting board and place a couple tablespoons of filling at one end. Roll the slice up and place it in the baking dish, seam-side down. Repeat with the remaining zucchini slices. Spoon the remaining sauce over the rolls and top with the Parmesan. 5. Bake. Bake the rolls for 30 to 35 minutes until the zucchini is tender and the cheese is golden. 6. Serve. Spoon the rolls onto four plates and serve them hot.

Per Serving:

calories: 342 | fat: 24g | protein: 20g | carbs: 14g | net carbs: 11g | fiber: 3g

Zucchini and Spinach Croquettes

Prep time: 9 minutes | Cook time: 7 minutes | Serves 6

- 4 eggs, slightly beaten
- ½ cup almond flour
- ½ cup goat cheese, crumbled
- 1 teaspoon fine sea salt
- 4 garlic cloves, minced
- 1 cup baby spinach

- ½ cup Parmesan cheese, grated
- ⅓ teaspoon red pepper flakes
- 1 pound (454 g) zucchini, peeled and grated
- ⅓ teaspoon dried dill weed

1. Thoroughly combine all ingredients in a bowl. Now, roll the mixture to form small croquettes. 2. Air fry at 340°F (171°C) for 7 minutes or until golden. Tate, adjust for seasonings and serve warm.

Per Serving:

calories: 179 | fat: 12g | protein: 11g | carbs: 6g | net carbs: 3g | fiber: 3g

Oven-Roasted Spaghetti Squash

Prep time: 10 minutes | Cook time: 45 minutes | Serves 6

- 1 (4 pounds / 1.8 kg) spaghetti squash, halved and seeded
- 2 tablespoons coconut oil

- 4 tablespoons salted butter, melted
- 1 teaspoon garlic powder
- 2 teaspoons dried parsley

1. Brush shell of spaghetti squash with coconut oil. Brush inside with butter. Sprinkle inside with garlic powder and parsley. 2. Place squash skin side down into ungreased air fryer basket, working in batches if needed. Adjust the temperature to 350°F (177°C) and set the timer for 30 minutes. When the timer beeps, flip squash and cook an additional 15 minutes until fork-tender. 3. Use a fork to remove spaghetti strands from shell and serve warm.

Per Serving:

calories: 210 | fat: 19g | protein: 2g | carbs: 11g | net carbs: 8g | fiber: 3g

Crunchy Cabbage Steaks

Prep time: 5 minutes | Cook time: 10 minutes | Serves 4

- 1 small head green cabbage, cored and cut into ½-inch-thick slices
- ¼ teaspoon salt
- ¼ teaspoon ground black pepper
- 2 tablespoons olive oil
- 1 clove garlic, peeled and finely minced
- ½ teaspoon dried thyme
- ½ teaspoon dried parsley

1. Sprinkle each side of cabbage with salt and pepper, then place into ungreased air fryer basket, working in batches if needed. 2. Drizzle each side of cabbage with olive oil, then sprinkle with remaining ingredients on both sides. Adjust the temperature to 350°F (177°C) and air fry for 10 minutes, turning "steaks" halfway through cooking. 3.Cabbage will be browned at the edges and tender when done. Serve warm.

Per Serving:

calories: 80 | fat:7g | protein: 1g | carbs: 5g | net carbs: 4g | fiber: 1g

Zucchini Boats with Three Cheeses

Prep time: 15 minutes | Cook time: 20 minutes | Serves 2

- 2 medium zucchini
- 1 tablespoon avocado oil
- ¼ cup low-carb, no-sugar-added pasta sauce
- ¼ cup full-fat ricotta cheese
- ¼ cup shredded Mozzarella cheese
- ¼ teaspoon dried oregano
- ¼ teaspoon garlic powder
- ½ teaspoon dried parsley
- 2 tablespoons grated vegetarian Parmesan cheese

1. Cut off 1 inch from the top and bottom of each zucchini. Slice zucchini in half lengthwise and use a spoon to scoop out a bit of the inside, making room for filling. Brush with oil and spoon 2 tablespoons pasta sauce into each shell. 2. In a medium bowl, mix ricotta, Mozzarella, oregano, garlic powder, and parsley. Spoon the mixture into each zucchini shell. Place stuffed zucchini shells into the air fryer basket. 3. Adjust the temperature to 350°F (177°C) and air fry for 20 minutes. 4. To remove from the basket, use tongs or a spatula and carefully lift out. Top with Parmesan. Serve immediately.

Per Serving:

calories: 245 | fat: 18g | protein: 12g | carbs: 9g | net carbs: 7g | fiber: 2g

Cheesy White Cheddar and Mushroom Soufflés

Prep time: 15 minutes | Cook time: 12 minutes | Serves 4

- 3 large eggs, whites and yolks separated
- ½ cup sharp white Cheddar cheese
- 3 ounces (85 g) cream cheese, softened
- ¼ teaspoon cream of tartar
- ¼ teaspoon salt
- ¼ teaspoon ground black pepper
- ½ cup cremini mushrooms, sliced

1. In a large bowl, whip egg whites until stiff peaks form, about 2 minutes. In a separate large bowl, beat Cheddar, egg yolks, cream cheese, cream of tartar, salt, and pepper together until combined. 2. Fold egg whites into cheese mixture, being careful not to stir. Fold in mushrooms, then pour mixture evenly into four ungreased ramekins. Place ramekins into air fryer basket. Adjust the temperature to 350°F (177°C) and bake for 12 minutes. Eggs will be browned on the top and firm in the center when done. Serve warm.

Per Serving:

calories: 228 | fat: 19g | protein: 13g | carbs: 2g | net carbs: 2g | fiber: 0g

Oven-Roasted Vegetable Bowl

Prep time: 10 minutes | Cook time: 15 minutes | Serves 2

- 1 cup broccoli florets
- 1 cup quartered Brussels sprouts
- ½ cup cauliflower florets
- ¼ medium white onion, peeled and sliced ¼ inch thick
- ½ medium green bell pepper, seeded and sliced ¼ inch thick
- 1 tablespoon coconut oil
- 2 teaspoons chili powder
- ½ teaspoon garlic powder
- ½ teaspoon cumin

1. Toss all ingredients together in a large bowl until vegetables are fully coated with oil and seasoning. 2. Pour vegetables into the air fryer basket. 3. Adjust the temperature to 360°F (182°C) and roast for 15 minutes. 4. Shake two or three times during cooking. Serve warm.

Per Serving:

calories: 168 | fat: 11g | protein: 4g | carbs: 15g | net carbs: 9g | fiber: 6g

Cauliflower Steak with Gremolata Sauce

Prep time: 15 minutes | Cook time: 25 minutes | Serves 4

- 2 tablespoons olive oil
- 1 tablespoon Italian seasoning
- 1 large head cauliflower, outer leaves removed and

Gremolata:

- 1 bunch Italian parsley (about 1 cup packed)
- 2 cloves garlic
- Zest of 1 small lemon, plus

sliced lengthwise through the core into thick "steaks"

- Salt and freshly ground black pepper, to taste
- ¼ cup Parmesan cheese

1 to 2 teaspoons lemon juice
- ½ cup olive oil
- Salt and pepper, to taste

1. Preheat the air fryer to 400ºF (204ºC). 2. In a small bowl, combine the olive oil and Italian seasoning. Brush both sides of each cauliflower "steak" generously with the oil. Season to taste with salt and black pepper. 3. Working in batches if necessary, arrange the cauliflower in a single layer in the air fryer basket. Pausing halfway through the cooking time to turn the "steaks," air fry for 15 to 20 minutes until the cauliflower is tender and the edges begin to brown. Sprinkle with the Parmesan and air fry for 5 minutes longer. 4. To make the gremolata: In a food processor fitted with a metal blade, combine the parsley, garlic, and lemon zest and juice. With the motor running, add the olive oil in a steady stream until the mixture forms a bright green sauce. Season to taste with salt and black pepper. Serve the cauliflower steaks with the gremolata spooned over the top.

Per Serving:

calories: 257 | fat: 23g | protein: 6g | carbs: 9g | net carbs: 7g | fiber: 4g

Nachos with Sweet Peppers

Prep time: 10 minutes | Cook time: 5 minutes | Serves 2

- 6 mini sweet peppers, seeded and sliced in half
- ¾ cup shredded Colby jack cheese
- ¼ cup sliced pickled

jalapeños
- ½ medium avocado, peeled, pitted, and diced
- 2 tablespoons sour cream

1. Place peppers into an ungreased round nonstick baking dish. Sprinkle with Colby and top with jalapeños. 2. Place dish into air fryer basket. Adjust the temperature to 350ºF (177ºC) and bake for 5 minutes. Cheese will be melted and bubbly when done. 3.

Remove dish from air fryer and top with avocado. Drizzle with sour cream. Serve warm.

Per Serving:

calories: 255 | fat: 21g | protein: 11g | carbs: 9g | net carbs: 5g | fiber: 4g

Hearty Eggplant and Zucchini Bites

Prep time: 30 minutes | Cook time: 30 minutes | Serves 8

- 2 teaspoons fresh mint leaves, chopped
- 1½ teaspoons red pepper chili flakes
- 2 tablespoons melted butter
- 1 pound (454 g) eggplant, peeled and cubed
- 1 pound (454 g) zucchini, peeled and cubed
- 3 tablespoons olive oil

1. Toss all the above ingredients in a large-sized mixing dish. 2. Roast the eggplant and zucchini bites for 30 minutes at 325ºF (163ºC) in your air fryer, turning once or twice. 3. Serve with a homemade dipping sauce.

Per Serving:

calories: 140 | fat: 12g | protein: 2g | carbs: 8g | net carbs: 6g | fiber: 2g

Peppers Stuffed with Quiche Filling

Prep time: 5 minutes | Cook time: 15 minutes | Serves 2

- 2 medium green bell peppers
- 3 large eggs
- ¼ cup full-fat ricotta cheese
- ¼ cup diced yellow onion
- ½ cup chopped broccoli
- ½ cup shredded medium Cheddar cheese

1. Cut the tops off of the peppers and remove the seeds and white membranes with a small knife. 2. In a medium bowl, whisk eggs and ricotta. 3. Add onion and broccoli. Pour the egg and vegetable mixture evenly into each pepper. Top with Cheddar. Place peppers into a 4-cup round baking dish and place into the air fryer basket. 4. Adjust the temperature to 350ºF (177ºC) and bake for 15 minutes. 5. Eggs will be mostly firm and peppers tender when fully cooked. Serve immediately.

Per Serving:

calories: 382 | fat: 27g | protein: 24g | carbs: 11g | net carbs: 7g | fiber: 4g

Mediterranean-Style Stuffed Eggplant

- 1 large eggplant
- 2 tablespoons unsalted butter
- ¼ medium yellow onion, diced
- ¼ cup chopped artichoke hearts
- 1 cup fresh spinach
- 2 tablespoons diced red bell pepper
- ½ cup crumbled feta

1. Slice eggplant in half lengthwise and scoop out flesh, leaving enough inside for shell to remain intact. Take eggplant that was scooped out, chop it, and set aside. 2. In a medium skillet over medium heat, add butter and onion. Sauté until onions begin to soften, about 3 to 5 minutes. Add chopped eggplant, artichokes, spinach, and bell pepper. Continue cooking 5 minutes until peppers soften and spinach wilts. Remove from the heat and gently fold in the feta. 3. Place filling into each eggplant shell and place into the air fryer basket. 4. Adjust the temperature to 320°F (160°C) and air fry for 20 minutes. 5. Eggplant will be tender when done. Serve warm.

Per Serving:

calories: 275 | fat: 20g | protein: 9g | carbs: 17g | net carbs: 13g | fiber: 4g

Asparagus and Fennel Egg Frittata

- 1 teaspoon coconut or regular butter, plus more for greasing
- 8 asparagus spears, diced
- ½ cup diced fennel
- ½ cup mushrooms, sliced (optional)
- 8 eggs
- ½ cup full-fat regular milk or coconut milk
- 1 tomato, sliced
- 1 teaspoon salt
- ½ teaspoon freshly ground black pepper
- Grated cheese (optional)

1. Preheat the oven to 350°F (180°C). Grease a pie dish with butter. 2. Melt 1 teaspoon of butter in a shallow skillet over medium-high heat and sauté the asparagus, fennel, and mushrooms (if using) for about 5 minutes, or until fork-tender. 3. Transfer the vegetables to the prepared pie dish. 4. Crack the eggs into a mixing bowl and pour in the milk. Whisk together until fully combined. 5. Pour the egg mixture over the vegetables in the pie dish, season with salt and pepper, and carefully and lightly mix everything together. Lay the tomato slices on top. 6. Bake the frittata for about 30 minutes. 7. Remove from the oven and let cool for 5 to 10 minutes. Slice into wedges and sprinkle with grated cheese, if desired.

Per Serving:

calories: 188 | fat: 12g | protein: 14g | carbs: 6g | net carbs: 4g | fiber: 2g

Parmesan-Crusted Artichokes

- 2 medium artichokes, trimmed and quartered, center removed
- 2 tablespoons coconut oil
- 1 large egg, beaten
- ½ cup grated vegetarian Parmesan cheese
- ¼ cup blanched finely ground almond flour
- ½ teaspoon crushed red pepper flakes

1. In a large bowl, toss artichokes in coconut oil and then dip each piece into the egg. 2. Mix the Parmesan and almond flour in a large bowl. Add artichoke pieces and toss to cover as completely as possible, sprinkle with pepper flakes. Place into the air fryer basket. 3. Adjust the temperature to 400°F (204°C) and air fry for 10 minutes. 4. Toss the basket two times during cooking. Serve warm.

Per Serving:

calories: 220 | fat: 18g | protein: 10g | carbs: 9g | net carbs: 4g | fiber: 5g

Simple Basic Spaghetti Squash

- ½ large spaghetti squash
- 1 tablespoon coconut oil
- 2 tablespoons salted butter,
- melted
- ½ teaspoon garlic powder
- 1 teaspoon dried parsley

1. Brush shell of spaghetti squash with coconut oil. Place the skin side down and brush the inside with butter. Sprinkle with garlic powder and parsley. 2. Place squash with the skin side down into the air fryer basket. 3. Adjust the temperature to 350°F (177°C) and air fry for 30 minutes. 4. Flip the squash so skin side is up and cook an additional 15 minutes or until fork tender. Serve warm.

Per Serving:

calories: 180 | fat: 17g | protein: 1g | carbs: 8g | net carbs: 5g | fiber: 3g

Baked Italian Egg and Vegetable Dish

Prep time: 10 minutes | Cook time: 10 minutes | Serves 2

- 2 tablespoons salted butter
- 1 small zucchini, sliced lengthwise and quartered
- ½ medium green bell pepper, seeded and diced
- 1 cup fresh spinach, chopped

- 1 medium Roma tomato, diced
- 2 large eggs
- ¼ teaspoon onion powder
- ¼ teaspoon garlic powder
- ½ teaspoon dried basil
- ¼ teaspoon dried oregano

1. Grease two ramekins with 1 tablespoon butter each. 2. In a large bowl, toss zucchini, bell pepper, spinach, and tomatoes. Divide the mixture in two and place half in each ramekin. 3. Crack an egg on top of each ramekin and sprinkle with onion powder, garlic powder, basil, and oregano. Place into the air fryer basket. 4. Adjust the temperature to 330ºF (166ºC) and bake for 10 minutes. 5. Serve immediately.

Per Serving:

calories: 260 | fat: 21g | protein: 10g | carbs: 8g | net carbs: 5g | fiber: 3g

Hearty Vegetarian Chili with Avocado

Prep time: 10 minutes | Cook time: 25 minutes | Serves 8

- 2 tablespoons good-quality olive oil
- ½ onion, finely chopped
- 1 red bell pepper, diced
- 2 jalapeño peppers, chopped
- 1 tablespoon minced garlic
- 2 tablespoons chili powder

- 1 teaspoon ground cumin
- 4 cups canned diced tomatoes
- 2 cups pecans, chopped
- 1 cup sour cream
- 1 avocado, diced
- 2 tablespoons chopped fresh cilantro

1. Sauté the vegetables. In a large pot over medium-high heat, warm the olive oil. Add the onion, red bell pepper, jalapeño peppers, and garlic and sauté until they've softened, about 4 minutes. Stir in the chili powder and cumin, stirring to coat the vegetables with the spices. 2. Cook the chili. Stir in the tomatoes and pecans and bring the chili to a boil, then reduce the heat to low and simmer until the vegetables are soft and the flavors mellow, about 20 minutes. 3. Serve. Ladle the chili into bowls and serve it with the sour cream, avocado, and cilantro.

Per Serving:

calories: 332 | fat: 32g | protein: 5g | carbs: 11g | net carbs: 5g | fiber: 6g

Layered Caprese Eggplant Stacks

Prep time: 5 minutes | Cook time: 12 minutes | Serves 4

- 1 medium eggplant, cut into ¼-inch slices
- 2 large tomatoes, cut into ¼-inch slices
- 4 ounces (113 g) fresh

- Mozzarella, cut into ½-ounce / 14-g slices
- 2 tablespoons olive oil
- ¼ cup fresh basil, sliced

1. In a baking dish, place four slices of eggplant on the bottom. Place a slice of tomato on top of each eggplant round, then Mozzarella, then eggplant. Repeat as necessary. 2. Drizzle with olive oil. Cover dish with foil and place dish into the air fryer basket. 3. Adjust the temperature to 350ºF (177ºC) and bake for 12 minutes. 4. When done, eggplant will be tender. Garnish with fresh basil to serve.

Per Serving:

calories: 203 | fat: 16g | protein: 8g | carbs: 10g | net carbs: 7g | fiber: 3g

Portobello Mushrooms Stuffed with Flavor

Prep time: 10 minutes | Cook time: 8 minutes | Serves 4

- 3 ounces (85 g) cream cheese, softened
- ½ medium zucchini, trimmed and chopped
- ¼ cup seeded and chopped red bell pepper
- 1½ cups chopped fresh

- spinach leaves
- 4 large portobello mushrooms, stems removed
- 2 tablespoons coconut oil, melted
- ½ teaspoon salt

1. In a medium bowl, mix cream cheese, zucchini, pepper, and spinach. 2. Drizzle mushrooms with coconut oil and sprinkle with salt. Scoop ¼ zucchini mixture into each mushroom. 3. Place mushrooms into ungreased air fryer basket. Adjust the temperature to 400ºF (204ºC) and air fry for 8 minutes. Portobellos will be tender and tops will be browned when done. Serve warm.

Per Serving:

calories: 157 | fat: 14g | protein: 4g | carbs: 5g | net carbs: 3g | fiber: 2g

Spinach and Cheese Pie without Crust

- 6 large eggs
- ¼ cup heavy whipping cream
- 1 cup frozen chopped spinach, drained
- 1 cup shredded sharp Cheddar cheese
- ¼ cup diced yellow onion

1. In a medium bowl, whisk eggs and add cream. Add remaining ingredients to bowl. 2. Pour into a round baking dish. Place into the air fryer basket. 3. Adjust the temperature to 320ºF (160ºC) and bake for 20 minutes. 4. Eggs will be firm and slightly browned when cooked. Serve immediately.

Per Serving:
calories: 263 | fat: 20g | protein: 18g | carbs: 4g | net carbs: 3g | fiber: 1g

Cauliflower in Tikka Masala Sauce

For The Cauliflower
- 1 head cauliflower, cut into small florets
- 1 tablespoon coconut oil, melted

For The Sauce
- 2 tablespoons coconut oil
- ½ onion, chopped
- 1 tablespoon minced garlic
- 1 tablespoon grated ginger
- 2 tablespoons garam masala

- 1 teaspoon ground cumin
- ½ teaspoon ground coriander

- 1 tablespoon tomato paste
- ½ teaspoon salt
- 1 cup crushed tomatoes
- 1 cup heavy (whipping) cream
- 1 tablespoon chopped fresh cilantro

Make The Cauliflower: 1. Preheat the oven. Set the oven temperature to 425°F. Line a baking sheet with aluminum foil. 2. Prepare the cauliflower. In a large bowl, toss the cauliflower with the coconut oil, cumin, and coriander. Spread the cauliflower on the baking sheet in a single layer and bake it for 20 minutes, until the cauliflower is tender. Make The Sauce: 1. Sauté the vegetables. While the cauliflower is baking, in a large skillet over medium-high heat, warm the coconut oil. Add the onion, garlic, and ginger and sauté until they've softened, about 3 minutes. 2. Finish the sauce. Stir in the garam masala, tomato paste, and salt until the vegetables are coated. Stir in the crushed tomatoes and bring to a boil, then reduce the heat to low and simmer the sauce for 10 minutes, stirring it often. Remove the skillet from the heat and stir in the cream and cilantro. 3. Assemble and serve. Add the cauliflower to the sauce, stirring to combine everything. Divide the mixture between four bowls and serve it hot.

Per Serving:
calories: 372 | fat: 32g | protein: 8g | carbs: 17g | net carbs: 10g | fiber: 7g

Stuffed Peppers with Cheese Filling

Prep time: 20 minutes | Cook time: 15 minutes | Serves 2

- 1 red bell pepper, top and seeds removed
- 1 yellow bell pepper, top and seeds removed
- Salt and pepper, to taste
- 1 cup Cottage cheese
- 4 tablespoons mayonnaise
- 2 pickles, chopped

1. Arrange the peppers in the lightly greased air fryer basket. Cook in the preheated air fryer at 400ºF (204ºC) for 15 minutes, turning them over halfway through the cooking time. 2. Season with salt and pepper. Then, in a mixing bowl, combine the cream cheese with the mayonnaise and chopped pickles. Stuff the pepper with the cream cheese mixture and serve. Enjoy!

Per Serving:
calories: 250 | fat: 20g | protein: 11g | carbs: 8g | net carbs: 6g | fiber: 2g

Broccoli in Garlic Sauce

Prep time: 19 minutes | Cook time: 15 minutes | Serves 4

- 2 tablespoons olive oil
- Kosher salt and freshly ground black pepper, to taste

Dipping Sauce:

- 2 teaspoons dried rosemary, crushed
- 3 garlic cloves, minced
- ⅓ teaspoon dried marjoram, crushed
- 1 pound (454 g) broccoli florets

- ¼ cup sour cream
- ⅓ cup mayonnaise

1. Lightly grease your broccoli with a thin layer of olive oil. Season with salt and ground black pepper. 2. Arrange the seasoned broccoli in the air fryer basket. Bake at 395ºF (202ºC) for 15 minutes, shaking once or twice. In the meantime, prepare the dipping sauce by mixing all the sauce ingredients. Serve warm broccoli with the dipping sauce and enjoy!

Per Serving:
calories: 250 | fat: 23g | protein: 3g | carbs: 10g | net carbs: 9g | fiber: 1g

Chapter 9

Desserts

Chocolate Cake with Walnuts

Prep time: 10 minutes | Cook time: 20 minutes | Serves 6

- 1 cup almond flour
- ⅔ cup Swerve
- ¼ cup unsweetened cocoa powder
- ¼ cup chopped walnuts
- 1 teaspoon baking powder
- 3 eggs
- ⅓ cup heavy (whipping) cream
- ¼ cup coconut oil
- Nonstick cooking spray

1. In a large bowl, combine the flour, Swerve, cocoa powder, walnuts, baking powder, eggs, cream, and coconut oil. Using a hand mixer on high speed, mix the ingredients until well incorporated and fluffy. This will help prevent the cake from being too dense. 2. Grease a heatproof pan, such as a 3-cup Bundt pan, with cooking spray. Pour the cake batter into the pan and cover it with aluminum foil. 3. Pour 2 cups of water into the inner cooking pot of the Instant Pot, then place a trivet inside the pot. Set the pan on the trivet. 4. Lock the lid into place. Select the Manual setting and adjust the pressure to High. Cook for 20 minutes. Once cooking is complete, allow the pressure to release naturally for 10 minutes, then perform a quick release for any remaining pressure. 5. Carefully remove the pan from the Instant Pot and let it cool for 15 to 20 minutes. Invert the cake onto a plate. It can be served hot or at room temperature. For an extra treat, serve with a dollop of whipped cream, if desired. Enjoy your delicious cake!

Per Serving:

calories: 240 | fat: 20g | protein: 5g | carbs: 10g | net carbs: 5g | fiber: 5g

Crustless Cheesecake Bites

Prep time: 10 minutes | Cook time: 30 minutes | Serves 4

- 4 ounces cream cheese, at room temperature
- ¼ cup sour cream
- 2 large eggs
- ⅓ cup Swerve natural sweetener
- ¼ teaspoon vanilla extract

1. Preheat the oven to 350°F (175°C). 2. In a medium mixing bowl, use a hand mixer to beat together the cream cheese, sour cream, eggs, sweetener, and vanilla extract until the mixture is smooth and well combined. 3. Place silicone liners (or cupcake paper liners) in the cups of a muffin tin. 4. Pour the cheesecake batter evenly into the liners, filling them about 2/3 full. Bake in the preheated oven for 30 minutes, or until the edges are set and the centers are slightly jiggly. 5. Once baked, remove the cheesecake bites from the oven and allow them to cool at room temperature. Then, refrigerate until completely cooled, about 3 hours. Store any extra cheesecake bites in a zip-top bag in the freezer for up to 3 months. Enjoy your delicious cheesecake bites!

Per Serving:

calories: 169 | fat: 15g | protein: 5g | carbs: 18g | net carbs: 2g | fiber: 0g

Coconut Lemon Squares

Prep time: 5 minutes | Cook time: 40 minutes | Serves 5 to 6

- 3 eggs
- 2 tablespoons grass-fed butter, softened
- ½ cup full-fat coconut milk
- ½ teaspoon baking powder
- ½ teaspoon vanilla extract
- ½ cup Swerve, or more to taste
- ¼ cup lemon juice
- 1 cup blanched almond flour

1. Begin by gathering all your ingredients. In a large mixing bowl, combine the eggs, melted butter, coconut milk, baking powder, vanilla extract, Swerve (or your preferred sweetener), lemon juice, and flour. Use a whisk or a hand mixer to blend the ingredients together thoroughly until the mixture is smooth and uniform in texture. This step is crucial for ensuring that all the flavors are well incorporated. 2. Next, prepare your Instant Pot by pouring 1 cup of filtered water into the inner pot. Insert the trivet, which will hold your dish above the water during cooking. Take a well-greased, Instant Pot-compatible pan or dish and carefully transfer the batter from the mixing bowl into it, ensuring an even distribution. 3. If you have a sling (a piece of foil or a silicone sling), you can use it to help lower the dish onto the trivet. Once the dish is in place, cover it loosely with aluminum foil to prevent condensation from dripping onto the batter. Close the lid of the Instant Pot, making sure the pressure release valve is set to the Sealing position. Select the Manual setting and adjust the cooking time to 40 minutes on High Pressure. 4. After the cooking cycle is complete, allow the Instant Pot to release pressure naturally for about 10 minutes. This helps to ensure that your dish remains moist and fluffy. After the 10 minutes have passed, carefully switch the pressure release valve to Venting to release any remaining steam. 5. Once the pressure has fully released, open the lid of the Instant Pot and carefully remove the dish using oven mitts, as it will be hot. Allow the dish to cool for a few minutes before cutting it into 6 equal squares. Serve your delicious creation warm, and enjoy every bite!

Per Serving:

calories: 166 | fat: 15g | protein: 6g | carbs: 3g | net carbs: 2g | fiber: 1g

No-Bake N'Oatmeal Chocolate Chip Cookies

Prep time: 20 minutes | Cook time: 0 minutes | Serves 14

- 1¼ cups (185 g) hulled hemp seeds
- ¼ cup (60 ml) melted coconut oil or cacao butter
- ½ teaspoon vanilla extract or powder
- ½ teaspoon ground cinnamon
- 2 drops liquid stevia
- ¼ cup (56 g) stevia-sweetened chocolate chips

1. Line a baking sheet with parchment paper or a silicone baking mat. 2. In a medium-sized bowl, combine the hemp seeds, coconut oil, vanilla, cinnamon, and stevia. Stir well to mix all the ingredients together. 3. Transfer the mixture to a blender or food processor and pulse lightly for about 1 second per pulse, three times. After the third pulse, pinch some of the dough with your fingers. If it holds together nicely, you're ready to move on. If not, pulse again until the dough holds together. 4. Gently fold the chocolate chips into the dough until evenly distributed. 5. Using a round tablespoon (or a 1-tablespoon cookie scoop/melon baller), scoop up the dough, packing it firmly into the tablespoon. Transfer each scoop to the prepared baking sheet. Repeat this process with the remaining dough, making a total of 14 cookies. 6. Chill the cookies in the refrigerator for 30 minutes before consuming. These cookies are best served chilled, straight from the fridge. Enjoy your delicious and nutritious treats!

Per Serving:

calories: 126 | fat: 11g | protein: 5g | carbs: 3g | net carbs: 1g | fiber: 2g

Peanut Butter Hemp Heart Cookies

Prep time: 10 minutes | Cook time: 14 minutes | Makes 1 dozen cookies

- ½ cup natural peanut butter, room temperature
- 1 large egg
- ½ cup hemp hearts
- ¼ cup granular erythritol
- ¼ teaspoon baking powder
- ½ teaspoon vanilla extract
- ½ cup sugar-free chocolate chips

1. Preheat the oven to 350°F (175°C) and line 2 baking sheets with parchment paper. 2. In a large mixing bowl, combine the peanut butter and egg using a whisk until smooth. Add the hemp hearts, erythritol, baking powder, and vanilla extract, and mix well using a wooden spoon. Gently fold in the chocolate chips until evenly distributed. 3. Using a cookie scoop or spoon, scoop 12 even-sized balls of dough onto the lined baking sheets, spacing them about 2 inches apart. Flatten each cookie slightly with a fork. 4. Bake the cookies for 12 to 14 minutes, or until they are golden brown and slightly firm to the touch. Allow the cookies to cool on the baking sheets for 10 minutes before handling, as they may fall apart if moved too soon. 5. Store any leftovers in a sealed container in the refrigerator for up to a week, or freeze for up to a month. Enjoy your delicious peanut butter cookies!

Per Serving:

calories: 120 | fat: 10g | protein: 6g | carbs: 4g | net carbs: 2g | fiber: 2g

Pecan Clusters

Prep time: 10 minutes | Cook time: 8 minutes | Serves 8

- 3 ounces (85 g) whole shelled pecans
- 1 tablespoon salted butter, melted
- 2 teaspoons confectioners'
- erythritol
- ½ teaspoon ground cinnamon
- ½ cup low-carb chocolate chips

1. In a medium bowl, toss the pecans with melted butter until well coated. Then, sprinkle the pecans with erythritol and cinnamon, mixing until evenly distributed. 2. Place the seasoned pecans into an ungreased air fryer basket. Adjust the temperature to 350°F (177°C) and air fry for 8 minutes, shaking the basket two times during cooking to ensure even roasting. The pecans will feel soft initially but will become crunchy as they cool. 3. While the pecans are air frying, line a large baking sheet with parchment paper. 4. In a medium microwave-safe bowl, place the chocolate. Microwave on high in 20-second increments, stirring in between, until the chocolate is completely melted and smooth. 5. Using a spoon, place 1 teaspoon of melted chocolate in a rounded mound on the parchment-lined baking sheet. Press 1 pecan into the top of each chocolate mound, repeating the process with the remaining chocolate and pecans. 6. Once all the clusters are formed, place the baking sheet in the refrigerator to cool for at least 30 minutes. Once cooled and set, store the clusters in a large sealed container in the refrigerator for up to 5 days. Enjoy your delicious chocolate-covered pecan clusters!

Per Serving:

calories: 104 | fat: 10g | protein: 1g | carbs: 3g | net carbs: 2g | fiber: 1g

Bacon Fudge

- ½ cup (70 g) bacon grease, melted
- ¼ cup (60 g) cacao butter
- ¼ cup (20 g) cacao powder
- 3 tablespoons
- confectioners'-style erythritol
- 1 teaspoon vanilla extract or powder
- ⅛ teaspoon finely ground gray sea salt

Special Equipment:

- Silicone mold with four 3-ounce (90-ml) cavities or a total volume capacity of 12 ounces (350 ml)

1. In a small bowl, combine all the ingredients and whisk continuously for about 5 minutes, or until the erythritol has fully dissolved and the mixture is smooth. 2. Pour the mixture into a silicone mold, ensuring it is evenly distributed. Place the mold in the refrigerator and let it firm up for 1 hour. 3. For the best texture and flavor, allow the fudge to soften at room temperature for about 30 minutes before enjoying. Enjoy your delicious homemade fudge!

Per Serving:

calories: 196 | fat: 18g | protein: 4g | carbs: 4g | net carbs: 2g | fiber: 2g

Coconut Flour Cake

- 2 tablespoons salted butter, melted
- ⅓ cup coconut flour
- 2 large eggs, whisked
- ½ cup granular erythritol
- 1 teaspoon baking powder
- 1 teaspoon vanilla extract
- ½ cup sour cream

1. In a large bowl, mix all the ingredients together until well combined. Once the batter is smooth, pour it into an ungreased round nonstick baking dish. 2. Place the baking dish into the air fryer basket. Set the temperature to 300ºF (149ºC) and bake for 25 minutes. The cake should turn a dark golden color on top, and a toothpick inserted into the center should come out clean when it's done. 3. After baking, let the cake cool in the dish for 15 minutes before slicing and serving. Enjoy your delicious air-fried cake!

Per Serving:

calories: 142 | fat: 10g | protein: 4g | carbs: 8g | net carbs: 4g | fiber: 4g

Egg Custard Tarts

- ¼ cup almond flour
- 1 tablespoon coconut oil
- 2 egg yolks
- ¼ cup coconut milk
- 1 tablespoon erythritol
- 1 teaspoon vanilla extract
- 1 cup water, for cooking

1. Make the dough by mixing almond flour and coconut oil in a bowl until well combined. 2. Press the dough into 2 mini tart molds, flattening it well to form cup shapes. 3. Pour water into the Instant Pot and insert the steamer rack. 4. Place the tart molds on the steamer rack in the Instant Pot. Close and seal the lid. 5. Cook the tarts for 3 minutes on Manual mode (High Pressure). After cooking, perform a quick pressure release. 6. In a separate bowl, whisk together the vanilla extract, erythritol, coconut milk, and egg yolks until smooth. 7. Carefully pour the liquid mixture into the tart molds. Close the lid of the Instant Pot again. 8. Cook the dessert for 7 minutes on Manual mode (High Pressure). 9. After the cooking time is complete, allow for a natural pressure release for an additional 10 minutes before opening the lid. Enjoy your delicious mini tarts!

Per Serving:

calories: 208 | fat: 20g | protein: 4g | carbs: 3g | net carbs: 2g | fiber: 1g

Instant Protein Ice Cream

- 1 cup unsweetened almond milk
- 1 scoop flavored protein powder of choice
- ¼ teaspoon xanthan gum
- 1½ cups ice
- Ground cinnamon, for garnish (optional)

1. Start by pouring the milk into a blender. Add the protein powder, xanthan gum, and ice. Blend on high for 20 to 30 seconds, or until the mixture is smooth and well combined. 2. Once blended, pour the mixture into a serving bowl. If desired, garnish with a dusting of cinnamon for added flavor. 3. Enjoy your protein-packed drink immediately!

Per Serving:

calories: 130 | fat: 5g | protein: 21g | carbs: 5g | net carbs: 3g | fiber: 2g

Coconut Muffins

Prep time: 5 minutes | Cook time: 25 minutes | Serves 5

- ½ cup coconut flour
- 2 tablespoons cocoa powder
- 3 tablespoons erythritol
- 1 teaspoon baking powder
- 2 tablespoons coconut oil
- 2 eggs, beaten
- ½ cup coconut shred

1. Start by combining all the ingredients in a mixing bowl, ensuring they are well mixed. 2. Next, pour the mixture into the molds of the muffin tin and carefully place them in the air fryer basket. 3. Cook the muffins at 350°F (177°C) for 25 minutes, or until they are cooked through and golden. Enjoy your delicious air-fried muffins!

Per Serving:

calories: 182 | fat: 14g | protein: 6g | carbs: 12g | net carbs: 5g | fiber: 7g

Orange–Olive Oil Cupcakes

Prep time: 15 minutes | Cook time: 20 minutes | Makes 6 cupcakes

- 1 large egg
- 2 tablespoons powdered sugar-free sweetener (such as stevia or monk fruit extract)
- ½ cup extra-virgin olive oil
- 1 teaspoon almond extract
- Zest of 1 orange
- 1 cup almond flour
- ¾ teaspoon baking powder
- ⅛ teaspoon salt
- 1 tablespoon freshly squeezed orange juice

1. Begin by preheating your oven to 350°F (180°C) and lining 6 cups of a muffin tin with muffin liners. 2. In a large mixing bowl, whisk together the egg and powdered sweetener until well combined. Then, add the olive oil, almond extract, and orange zest, continuing to whisk until the mixture is smooth and cohesive. 3. In a separate small bowl, combine the almond flour, baking powder, and salt, whisking them together. Gradually add this dry mixture to the wet ingredients, along with the orange juice, stirring gently until just combined—be careful not to overmix. 4. Evenly distribute the batter into the prepared muffin cups, filling each one. Bake in the preheated oven for 15 to 18 minutes, or until a toothpick inserted into the center of a muffin comes out clean. 5. Once baked, remove the muffins from the oven and let them cool in the tin for about 5 minutes before transferring them to a wire rack to cool completely. Enjoy your delightful muffins!

Per Serving:

1 cup cake: calories: 280 | fat: 27g | protein: 4g | carbs: 8g | net carbs: 6g | fiber: 2g

Vanilla Cream Pie

Prep time: 20 minutes | Cook time: 35 minutes | Serves 12

- 1 cup heavy cream
- 3 eggs, beaten
- 1 teaspoon vanilla extract
- ¼ cup erythritol
- 1 cup coconut flour
- 1 tablespoon butter, melted
- 1 cup water, for cooking

1. In a mixing bowl, combine coconut flour, erythritol, vanilla extract, eggs, and heavy cream until well mixed. 2. Grease a baking pan with melted butter to prevent sticking. 3. Pour the coconut mixture into the prepared baking pan. 4. Add water to the Instant Pot and insert the steamer rack. 5. Carefully place the baking pan on the rack, then close and seal the lid of the Instant Pot. 6. Set the Instant Pot to Manual mode (High Pressure) and cook the pie for 35 minutes. 7. Once the cooking time is complete, allow for a natural pressure release for 10 minutes before opening the lid. Enjoy your delicious coconut pie!

Per Serving:

calories: 100 | fat: 7g | protein: 3g | carbs: 12g | net carbs: 8g | fiber: 4g

Peanut Butter Cookies

Prep time: 5 minutes | Cook time: 10 minutes | Makes 15 cookies

- 1 cup natural crunchy peanut butter
- ½ cup Swerve natural
- sweetener
- 1 egg

1. Begin by preheating your oven to 350°F and lining a baking sheet with a silicone baking mat or parchment paper. 2. In a medium bowl, use a hand mixer to combine the peanut butter, sweetener, and egg until well mixed. 3. Roll the batter into small balls, approximately 1 inch in diameter. 4. Place the cookie dough balls on the prepared baking sheet, then flatten each ball with the tines of a fork, creating a crisscross pattern by pressing down in two directions. 5. Bake the cookies in the preheated oven for about 12 minutes, or until they turn golden. 6. Allow the cookies to cool on the lined pan for 10 minutes before serving, as they may crumble if moved too soon. 7. Store any leftover cookies in the refrigerator, covered, for up to 5 days. Enjoy your delicious peanut butter cookies!

Per Serving:

calories: 98 | fat: 8g | protein: 4g | carbs: 10g | net carbs: 3g | fiber: 1g

Candied Mixed Nuts

Prep time: 5 minutes | Cook time: 15 minutes | Serves 8

- 1 cup pecan halves
- 1 cup chopped walnuts
- ⅓ cup Swerve, or more to taste
- ⅓ cup grass-fed butter
- 1 teaspoon ground cinnamon

1. Preheat your oven to 350ºF (180ºC) and line a baking sheet with aluminum foil. 2. While the oven is warming up, pour ½ cup of filtered water into the inner pot of the Instant Pot. Add the pecans, walnuts, Swerve, butter, and cinnamon to the pot. Stir the nut mixture to combine. Close the lid and set the pressure valve to Sealing. Use the Manual mode to cook at High Pressure for 5 minutes. 3. Once the cooking time is complete, perform a quick release by carefully switching the pressure valve to Venting. After releasing the pressure, strain the nuts to remove excess liquid. Pour the nuts onto the prepared baking sheet, spreading them out in an even layer. Place the baking sheet in the oven and bake for 5 to 10 minutes, or until the nuts are crisp, being careful not to overcook them. Allow the nuts to cool before serving. Store any leftovers in the refrigerator or freezer for later enjoyment.

Per Serving:

calories: 122 | fat: 12g | protein: 4g | carbs: 3g | net carbs: 1g | fiber: 2g

Snickerdoodle Cream Cheesecake

Prep time: 5 minutes | Cook time: 90 minutes | Serves 1

Filling:
- 1 tablespoon cream cheese, room temperature
- 1 teaspoon powdered

Cake:
- 1½ tablespoons coconut flour
- 1 tablespoon golden flax meal
- ¼ teaspoon baking powder
- ⅛ teaspoon cream of tartar

For Garnish (optional):
- Ground cinnamon

- erythritol
- 1 teaspoon ground cinnamon

- 2 tablespoons unsalted butter, melted but not hot
- 1 large egg
- ½ teaspoon vanilla extract
- ¼ teaspoon plus 15 drops of liquid stevia

- Powdered erythritol

1. To prepare the filling, start by placing a piece of plastic wrap in a

small bowl. Add the cream cheese, erythritol, and cinnamon to the center of the wrap. Use a spoon to mix the ingredients together until well combined, then gather the plastic wrap around the mixture to securely enclose it. With your hands, shape the filling into a small disc, approximately 1 inch in diameter and ½ inch thick. Place this disc in the freezer for 30 minutes to firm up. 2. While the filling is chilling, make the cake batter. In a separate small bowl, use a fork to whisk together the coconut flour, flax meal, baking powder, and cream of tartar. In another bowl, combine the melted butter, egg, vanilla extract, and stevia, whisking until smooth. 3. Gradually add the dry mixture to the wet mixture, whisking continuously until you achieve a thick, batter-like consistency. 4. Next, grease a 4- or 5-ounce microwave-safe ramekin with coconut oil spray. Pour half of the prepared batter into the ramekin. Remove the cream cheese disc from the freezer, unwrap it, and place it in the center of the batter in the ramekin. Gently press it down, ensuring it doesn't touch the bottom. Pour the remaining batter on top of the filling, spreading it evenly to fully cover the disc. 5. Microwave the ramekin for 90 seconds. Once done, carefully flip the cake onto a plate. If desired, dust the top with ground cinnamon and powdered erythritol before serving. Enjoy your delicious treat!

Per Serving:

calories: 403 | fat: 36g | protein: 11g | carbs: 12g | net carbs: 5g | fiber: 7g

Pecan Brownies

Prep time: 10 minutes | Cook time: 20 minutes | Serves 6

- ½ cup blanched finely ground almond flour
- ½ cup powdered erythritol
- 2 tablespoons unsweetened cocoa powder
- ½ teaspoon baking powder
- ¼ cup unsalted butter, softened
- 1 large egg
- ¼ cup chopped pecans
- ¼ cup low-carb, sugar-free chocolate chips

1. In a large bowl, combine almond flour, erythritol, cocoa powder, and baking powder, then stir in the melted butter and egg until well mixed. 2. Gently fold in the pecans and chocolate chips, then scoop the mixture into a round baking pan. Place the pan into the air fryer basket. 3. Set the air fryer temperature to 300ºF (149ºC) and bake for 20 minutes. 4. To check for doneness, insert a toothpick into the center; it should come out clean when fully cooked. Allow the baked good to cool for 20 minutes to firm up before serving. Enjoy your delicious treat!

Per Serving:

calories: 218 | fat: 20g | protein: 4g | carbs: 10g | net carbs: 4g | fiber: 6g

Crustless Creamy Berry Cheesecake

Prep time: 10 minutes | Cook time: 40 minutes | Serves 12

- 16 ounces (454 g) cream cheese, softened
- 1 cup powdered erythritol
- ¼ cup sour cream
- 2 teaspoons vanilla extract
- 2 eggs
- 2 cups water
- ¼ cup blackberries and strawberries, for topping

1. In a large mixing bowl, beat the cream cheese and erythritol together until the mixture is smooth and creamy. Add the sour cream, vanilla extract, and eggs, and gently fold them into the cream cheese mixture until everything is well combined. 2. Pour the batter into a 7-inch springform pan, ensuring it is evenly distributed. Gently shake or tap the pan on the counter to remove any air bubbles and to level the batter. Cover the top of the pan with aluminum foil to prevent excess moisture from entering. Pour water into the Instant Pot and place the steam rack inside. 3. Carefully lower the springform pan onto the steam rack in the Instant Pot. Press the Cake button, then press the Adjust button to set the heat to More. Set the cooking time for 40 minutes. Once the timer beeps, allow the Instant Pot to release pressure naturally. Using a sling or a pair of tongs, carefully lift the pan out of the Instant Pot and let it cool completely before placing it in the refrigerator. 4. Once the cheesecake has chilled, arrange fresh strawberries and blackberries on top for a decorative and delicious finish. Serve and enjoy your homemade cheesecake.

Per Serving:

calories: 153 | fat: 13g | protein: 3g | carbs: 14g | net carbs: 14g | fiber: 0g

Keto Brownies

Prep time: 15 minutes | Cook time: 15 minutes | Serves 8

- 1 cup coconut flour
- 1 tablespoon cocoa powder
- 1 tablespoon coconut oil
- 1 teaspoon vanilla extract
- 1 teaspoon baking powder
- 1 teaspoon apple cider vinegar
- ⅓ cup butter, melted
- 1 tablespoon erythritol
- 1 cup water, for cooking

1. In a mixing bowl, combine erythritol, melted butter, apple cider vinegar, baking powder, vanilla extract, coconut oil, cocoa powder, and coconut flour. Mix thoroughly until all ingredients are well incorporated. 2. Whisk the mixture until it becomes smooth, then pour it into a baking pan, ensuring the surface of the batter is evenly flattened. 3. Pour water into the Instant Pot and insert the steamer rack. 4. Place the pan with the brownie batter onto the steamer rack inside the Instant Pot. Close and seal the lid securely. 5. Set the Instant Pot to Manual mode (High Pressure) and cook the brownies for 15 minutes. 6. After cooking, allow the pressure to release naturally for 5 minutes before opening the lid. 7. Once the brownies are cooked and slightly cooled, cut them into bars and serve.

Per Serving:

calories: 146 | fat: 11g | protein: 2g | carbs: 9g | net carbs: 5g | fiber: 4g

Almond Chai Truffles

Prep time: 200 minutes | Cook time: 0 minutes | Serves 10

- ½ cup (140 g) unsweetened smooth almond butter
- ¼ cup plus 2 tablespoons (90 g) cacao butter, melted
- 1 tablespoon plus 1 teaspoon chai spice (recipe below)
- 1 tablespoon confectioners'-
- style erythritol or 2 to 4 drops liquid stevia ½ teaspoon vanilla extract or powder
- Pinch of finely ground gray sea salt
- 3 tablespoons almonds, roasted

Special Equipment:

- 10 mini paper liners (optional)

1. In a medium-sized bowl, combine almond butter, cacao butter, chai spice, erythritol, vanilla, and salt, stirring until well mixed. Place the mixture in the fridge to set for 30 to 45 minutes, until it is firm yet still pliable. 2. While the mixture sets, place the roasted almonds in a small baggie, seal it, and cover with a kitchen towel. Use a mallet or the bottom of a mug to bash the almonds until the pieces are no larger than ⅛ inch (3 mm), then pour them into a small bowl. 3. Line a rimmed baking sheet with parchment paper or a silicone baking mat. 4. Once the truffle mixture is ready, break it up with a fork until no clumps larger than a pencil eraser remain. Scoop a tablespoon of the mixture and roll it quickly between your palms, then place it in the bowl with the roasted almond pieces and toss to coat. After coating, transfer the truffle to the prepared baking sheet. Clean your hands to avoid transferring almond pieces to the truffle mixture, and repeat with the remaining dough to make a total of 10 truffles. 5. Serve the truffles in mini paper liners if desired; they are best enjoyed at room temperature. Enjoy your delicious truffles!

Per Serving:

calories: 196 | fat: 18g | protein: 4g | carbs: 4g | net carbs: 2g | fiber: 2g

Double Chocolate Brownies

- 1 cup almond flour
- ½ cup unsweetened cocoa powder
- ½ teaspoon baking powder
- ⅓ cup Swerve
- ¼ teaspoon salt
- ½ cup unsalted butter, melted and cooled
- 3 eggs
- 1 teaspoon vanilla extract
- 2 tablespoons mini semisweet chocolate chips

1. Preheat the air fryer to 350ºF (177ºC) and line a cake pan with parchment paper, brushing it lightly with oil. 2. In a large bowl, mix together the almond flour, cocoa powder, baking powder, Swerve, and salt. Then, add the butter, eggs, and vanilla, stirring until the mixture is thoroughly combined; the batter will be thick. Spread the batter evenly into the prepared pan and scatter chocolate chips on top. 3. Air fry the brownies for 15 to 20 minutes, or until the edges are set while the center remains slightly undercooked. Allow the brownies to cool completely before slicing. To store, cover and refrigerate for up to 3 days. Enjoy your delicious brownies!

Per Serving:
calories: 191 | fat: 17g | protein: 6g | carbs: 7g | net carbs: 3g | fiber: 4g

Fruit Pizza

Crust:
- 1¼ cups finely ground blanched almond flour
- ⅓ cup granular erythritol
- 1 teaspoon baking powder

Toppings:
- 5 ounces cream cheese (½ cup plus 2 tablespoons), softened
- 2 tablespoons granular erythritol
- 1 tablespoon heavy
- 1 large egg
- 5 tablespoons salted butter, softened
- 1 teaspoon vanilla extract

whipping cream
- ½ cup sliced fresh strawberries or whole raspberries
- ½ cup fresh blueberries

1. Preheat your oven to 350°F (175°C) and grease the bottom of a 9-inch springform pan to ensure easy removal of the crust later. 2. To make the crust, start by whisking together the almond flour, erythritol, and baking powder in a small bowl. In a separate medium-sized bowl, whisk the egg, then add in the melted butter and vanilla extract, mixing until well combined. Gradually incorporate the dry flour mixture into the wet ingredients, stirring until a cohesive dough forms. 3. Evenly spread the crust mixture into the prepared springform pan, pressing it down to form an even layer. Bake the crust for 12 to 14 minutes, or until it is lightly browned on top and around the edges. Once baked, allow the crust to cool completely before removing it from the pan. 4. While the crust is cooling, prepare the topping. In a small bowl, use a spoon to beat together the cream cheese, erythritol, and heavy cream until the mixture is smooth and fully combined. Once the crust has cooled, spread the cream cheese mixture evenly over the top. Garnish with fresh berries of your choice for added flavor and visual appeal. 5. Cover the dessert and refrigerate it for at least 2 hours to allow the flavors to meld and the topping to set. Any leftovers can be stored in an airtight container in the refrigerator for up to 2 days, ensuring they remain fresh and delicious.

Per Serving:
calories: 230 | fat: 20g | protein: 6g | carbs: 5g | net carbs: 3g | fiber: 2g

Berry Cheesecake Fat Bomb

- 4 ounces cream cheese, at room temperature
- 4 tablespoons (½ stick) butter, at room temperature
- 2 teaspoons Swerve natural
- sweetener or 2 drops liquid stevia
- 1 teaspoon vanilla extract
- ¼ cup berries, fresh or frozen

1. In a medium bowl, use a hand mixer to beat together the cream cheese, butter, sweetener, and vanilla extract until the mixture is smooth and creamy. 2. In a small bowl, thoroughly mash the berries until they reach a jam-like consistency. Gently fold the mashed berries into the cream cheese mixture using a rubber scraper, ensuring they are evenly distributed. (It's important to mash the berries well to avoid an unpleasant texture when frozen.) 3. Spoon the cream cheese mixture into fat bomb molds. If you don't have specific molds, you can use small silicone cupcake molds placed in the cups of a muffin tin, or simply use cupcake papers. 4. Place the molds in the freezer and let them freeze for at least 2 hours. Once they are fully frozen, unmold the fat bombs and enjoy! Any leftover fat bombs can be stored in a zip-top bag in the freezer for up to 3 months. It's convenient to have some on hand for when you crave a sweet treat.

Per Serving:
calories: 414 | fat: 43g | protein: 4g | carbs: 9g | net carbs: 4g | fiber: 1g

Crustless Peanut Butter Cheesecake

Prep time: 10 minutes | Cook time: 10 minutes | Serves 2

- 4 ounces (113 g) cream cheese, softened
- 2 tablespoons confectioners' erythritol
- 1 tablespoon all-natural, no-sugar-added peanut butter
- ½ teaspoon vanilla extract
- 1 large egg, whisked

1. In a medium bowl, mix the cream cheese and erythritol until smooth, then add the peanut butter and vanilla, continuing to mix until well combined. Stir in the egg just until incorporated. 2. Spoon the mixture into an ungreased springform pan and place it in the air fryer basket. Set the temperature to 300ºF (149ºC) and bake for 10 minutes; the edges should be firm while the center remains mostly set with a slight jiggle. 3. Allow the pan to cool at room temperature for 30 minutes, then cover it with plastic wrap and refrigerate for at least 2 hours. Serve chilled and enjoy your delicious cheesecake!

Per Serving:

calories: 281 | fat: 26g | protein: 8g | carbs: 4g | net carbs: 4g | fiber: 0g

Baked Cheesecake

Prep time: 30 minutes | Cook time: 35 minutes | Serves 6

- ½ cup almond flour
- 1½ tablespoons unsalted butter, melted
- 2 tablespoons erythritol
- 1 (8 ounces / 227 g) package

Topping:
- 1½ cups sour cream
- 3 tablespoons powdered
- cream cheese, softened
- ¼ cup powdered erythritol
- ½ teaspoon vanilla paste
- 1 egg, at room temperature

- erythritol
- 1 teaspoon vanilla extract

1. In a mixing bowl, thoroughly combine the almond flour, butter, and 2 tablespoons of erythritol. Press this mixture into the bottom of lightly greased custard cups to form the crust. 2. Using an electric mixer on low speed, blend the cream cheese, ¼ cup of powdered erythritol, vanilla, and egg until smooth. Pour this batter over the crust in the custard cups. 3. Preheat your air fryer to 330ºF (166ºC) and bake the custard cups for 35 minutes, or until the edges are puffed and the surface is firm. 4. For the topping, mix the sour cream, 3 tablespoons of powdered erythritol, and vanilla together. Spread this mixture over the cooled crust. 5. Allow the custard cups to cool to room temperature, then transfer them to the refrigerator for 6 to 8 hours. Serve chilled.

Per Serving:

calories: 290 | fat: 27g | protein: 6g | carbs: 7g | net carbs: 4g | fiber: 3g

Raspberry Cheesecake

Prep time: 10 minutes | Cook time: 25 to 30 minutes | Serves 12

- ⅔ cup coconut oil, melted
- ½ cup cream cheese, at room temperature
- 6 eggs
- 3 tablespoons granulated
- sweetener
- 1 teaspoon alcohol-free pure vanilla extract
- ½ teaspoon baking powder
- ¾ cup raspberries

1. Preheat your oven to 350°F (175°C). Line an 8-by-8-inch baking dish with parchment paper and set it aside. 2. In a large mixing bowl, beat together the coconut oil and cream cheese until the mixture is smooth and well combined. 3. Add the eggs to the bowl and continue to beat, making sure to scrape down the sides of the bowl at least once to incorporate all the ingredients. 4. Next, mix in the sweetener, vanilla extract, and baking powder, beating until the batter is smooth and uniform. 5. Spoon the batter into the prepared baking dish and use a spatula to smooth out the top evenly. Scatter the raspberries over the top of the batter. 6. Bake in the preheated oven until the center is firm, which should take about 25 to 30 minutes. 7. Once baked, allow the cheesecake to cool completely in the baking dish before cutting it into 12 squares. Enjoy your delicious raspberry cheesecake squares!

Per Serving:

1 square: calories: 176 | fat: 18g | protein: 6g | carbs: 3g | net carbs: 2g | fiber: 1g

Toasted Coconut Marshmallows

- ½ cup (50 g) toasted unsweetened shredded coconut, divided
- 1 cup (240 ml) water, divided
- 3 tablespoons unflavored gelatin
- 1 cup (160 g) confectioners'-style erythritol
- 2 teaspoons vanilla extract
- ¼ teaspoon finely ground gray sea salt

1. Begin by lining an 8-inch (20-cm) square pan with parchment paper, allowing the ends to drape over the sides for easy lifting later. Sprinkle ¼ cup (25 g) of the toasted coconut into the pan, spreading it evenly across the bottom. 2. Attach the whisk attachment to your hand mixer or stand mixer. 3. In the bowl of your mixer, pour in ½ cup (120 ml) of water and sprinkle the gelatin on top. Do not stir; just let it sit while you prepare the other ingredients. 4. In a small saucepan, combine the remaining ½ cup (120 ml) of water, erythritol, vanilla extract, and salt. Heat the mixture over medium heat, stirring occasionally until it reaches a rapid boil. Be careful to monitor it to prevent it from spilling over. Once it begins to boil, remove it from the heat and reduce the heat to low, allowing it to maintain a low boil for 5 minutes. 5. Carefully transfer the hot liquid to the bowl with the gelatin mixture. Turn the mixer to high speed and beat for 6 to 7 minutes, or until the mixture thickens to a spreadable consistency, similar to marshmallow fluff. Be cautious not to overbeat, as it will become too stiff to spread easily. 6. Once thickened, pour the marshmallow fluff into the prepared pan and sprinkle the remaining ¼ cup (25 g) of toasted coconut on top. 7. Use the back of a spatula to smooth the marshmallow fluff evenly in the pan. Alternatively, you can grease your palms with a small amount of coconut oil and spread the fluff with your hands. 8. Allow the marshmallows to sit at room temperature for 1 to 2 hours until they are firm. Once set, cut them into 1-inch (2.5-cm) squares and enjoy your delicious homemade marshmallows!

Per Serving:
calories: 30 | fat: 2g | protein: 2g | carbs: 1g | net carbs: 0g | fiber: 1g

Coconut Chocolate Cookies

- ¼ cup (½ stick) unsalted butter, room temperature
- 1 ounce cream cheese (2 tablespoons), room temperature
- ¼ cup plus 2 tablespoons powdered erythritol
- 1 large egg
- ¼ cup heavy whipping cream
- ¼ cup coconut flour
- ¼ cup cocoa powder
- ½ teaspoon baking powder
- ¼ teaspoon pink Himalayan salt
- ½ cup unsweetened coconut flakes

1. Preheat your oven to 325°F (163°C) and line two baking sheets with parchment paper to prevent the cookies from sticking and to make cleanup easier. 2. In a large bowl, use a hand mixer to cream together the butter, cream cheese, and erythritol until the mixture is light and fluffy. Add in the egg and heavy cream, mixing until well combined. Set this mixture aside. 3. In a small bowl, whisk together the coconut flour, cocoa powder, baking powder, and salt. Gradually add the dry mixture to the wet ingredients in two batches, mixing with the hand mixer after each addition until you achieve a soft, slightly crumbly dough. Gently fold in the coconut flakes to evenly distribute them throughout the dough. 4. Using a cookie scoop or a spoon, scoop out 12 even-sized balls of dough and place them onto the lined baking sheets. Flatten each ball with a fork to your desired thickness, as the cookies will not spread during baking. Bake the cookies for 15 minutes, or until they are slightly firm to the touch. Allow the cookies to cool on the baking sheets for 20 minutes before handling them, as they will be fragile and may fall apart if moved too soon. 5. Once cooled, store the cookies in a sealed container to maintain their freshness. They can be kept at room temperature or in the refrigerator, depending on your preference. Enjoy your delicious, homemade cookies!

Per Serving:
calories: 91 | fat: 8g | protein: 1g | carbs: 3g | net carbs: 1g | fiber: 2g

Chapter 10

Stews and Soups

Savory Mushroom Pizza Soup

- 1 teaspoon coconut oil
- ¼ cup cremini mushrooms, sliced
- 5 ounces (142 g) Italian sausages, chopped
- ½ jalapeño pepper, sliced
- ½ teaspoon Italian seasoning
- 1 teaspoon unsweetened tomato purée
- 1 cup water
- 4 ounces (113 g) Mozzarella, shredded

1. Melt the coconut oil in the Instant Pot on Sauté mode. 2. Add the mushrooms and cook for 10 minutes. 3. Add the chopped sausages, sliced jalapeño, Italian seasoning, and unsweetened tomato purée. Pour in the water and stir to mix well. 4. Close the lid and select Manual mode. Set cooking time for 12 minutes on High Pressure. 5. When timer beeps, use a quick pressure release and open the lid. 6. Ladle the soup in the bowls. Top it with Mozzarella. Serve warm.

Per Serving:

calories: 289 | fat: 23g | protein: 18g | carbs: 3g | net carbs: 2g | fiber: 0g

Budget-Friendly Pumpkin Soup

- 2 (9 ounces) packages soy chorizo
- 6 cups chicken bone broth
- ½ (15 ounces) can pure pumpkin
- 2 cups cooked riced cauliflower
- 1 cup unsweetened coconut milk
- 1 teaspoon garlic powder
- 1 teaspoon ground cinnamon
- 1 teaspoon ground ginger
- 1 teaspoon ground nutmeg
- 1 teaspoon paprika
- ⅛ teaspoon salt
- ⅛ teaspoon black pepper

1. Place a medium soup pot over medium heat and add all ingredients. Bring to boil while stirring regularly (5 to 10 minutes). 2. Reduce heat. Let simmer 15 minutes, stirring regularly until desired consistency achieved. 3. Remove from heat, let cool 5 minutes, and serve.

Per Serving:

calories: 237| fat: 15g | protein: 17g | carbs: 13g | net carbs: 8g | fiber: 5g

Cheddar and Sausage Beer Soup

- 1 cup heavy cream
- 10 ounces sausages, sliced
- 1 cup celery, chopped
- 1 cup carrots, chopped
- 4 garlic cloves, minced
- 8 ounces cream cheese
- 1 teaspoon red pepper flakes
- 6 ounces beer
- 16 ounces beef stock
- 1 onion, diced
- 1 cup cheddar cheese, grated
- Salt and black pepper, to taste
- Fresh cilantro, chopped, to garnish

1. Turn on the slow cooker. Add beef stock, beer, sausages, carrots, onion, garlic, celery, salt, red pepper flakes, and black pepper, and stir to combine. Pour in enough water to cover all the ingredients by roughly 2 inches. Close the lid and cook for 6 hours on Low. 2. Open the lid and stir in the heavy cream, cheddar, and cream cheese, and cook for 2 more hours. Ladle the soup into bowls and garnish with cilantro before serving. Yummy!

Per Serving:

calories: 387| fat: 28g | protein: 24g | carbs: 12g | net carbs: 9g | fiber: 2g

Broccoli Cheese Soup

- 8 cups chicken broth
- 2 large heads broccoli, chopped into bite-sized florets
- 1 clove garlic, peeled and minced
- ¼ cup heavy whipping cream
- ¼ cup shredded Cheddar cheese
- ⅛ teaspoon salt
- ⅛ teaspoon black pepper

1. In a medium pot over medium heat, add broth and bring to boil (about 5 minutes). Add broccoli and garlic. Reduce heat to low, cover pot, and simmer until vegetables are fully softened, about 15 minutes. 2. Remove from heat and blend using a hand immersion blender to desired consistency while still in pot. Leave some chunks of varying sizes for variety. 3. Return pot to medium heat and add cream and cheese. Stir 3 to 5 minutes until fully blended. Add salt and pepper. 4. Remove from heat, let cool 10 minutes, and serve.

Per Serving:

calories: 82 | fat: 4g | protein: 5g | carbs: 8g | net carbs: 5g | fiber: 3g

Creamy Cauliflower Soup

Prep time: 10 minutes | Cook time: 6 minutes | Serves 4

- 2 cups chopped cauliflower
- 2 tablespoons fresh cilantro
- 1 cup coconut cream
- 2 cups beef broth
- 3 ounces (85 g) Provolone cheese, chopped

1. Put cauliflower, cilantro, coconut cream, beef broth, and cheese in the Instant Pot. Stir to mix well. 2. Select Manual mode and set cooking time for 6 minutes on High Pressure. 3. When timer beeps, allow a natural pressure release for 4 minutes, then release any remaining pressure. Open the lid. 4. Blend the soup and ladle in bowls to serve.

Per Serving:
calories: 244 | fat: 21g | protein: 10g | carbs: 7g | net carbs: 4g | fiber: 3g

Avocado-Lime Soup with Mixed Herbs and Veggies

Prep time: 5 minutes | Cook time: 20 minutes | serves 8

- 2 tablespoons cold-pressed olive oil
- ½ yellow onion, chopped
- 1 teaspoon ground cumin
- 1 teaspoon ground coriander
- 1 teaspoon chili powder
- ¼ cup hemp hearts
- 1 medium tomato, chopped
- 1 cup chopped cabbage (set some aside for garnish)
- ½ cup chopped fresh cilantro
- ½ cup chopped celery
- ½ jalapeño pepper, chopped
- 8 cups vegetable broth
- Juice of 2 limes
- 1 avocado, peeled, pitted, and cut into cubes
- 3 flax crackers

1. Heat the olive oil in a large stockpot over medium heat and add the onion, cumin, coriander, and chili powder. Sauté, stirring occasionally, until the onion becomes tender, about 5 minutes. 2. Add the hemp hearts, tomato, cabbage, cilantro, celery, and jalapeño to the pot. Stir to coat the spices and allow to cook for 4 minutes. 3. Pour the broth into the pot and simmer on low for 20 minutes. 4. Remove the pot from the heat and stir in the lime juice. 5. Divide the avocado equally among 4 serving bowls. 6. Pour the soup over the avocado in the bowls and garnish with additional cabbage and cilantro. 7. Break the flax crackers over the top of the soup to create a "tortilla soup" vibe.

Per Serving:
calories: 130 | fat: 9g | protein: 3g | carbs: 9g | net carbs: 5g | fiber: 4g

Hearty Green Minestrone Soup

Prep time: 10 minutes | Cook time: 20 minutes | Serves 4

- 2 tablespoons ghee
- 2 tablespoons onion-garlic puree
- 2 heads broccoli, cut in florets
- 2 stalks celery, chopped
- 5 cups vegetable broth
- 1 cup baby spinach
- Salt and black pepper to taste
- 2 tablespoons Gruyere cheese, grated

1. Melt the ghee in a saucepan over medium heat and sauté the onion-garlic puree for 3 minutes until softened. Mix in the broccoli and celery, and cook for 4 minutes until slightly tender. Pour in the broth, bring to a boil, then reduce the heat to medium-low and simmer covered for about 5 minutes. 2. Drop in the spinach to wilt, adjust the seasonings, and cook for 4 minutes. Ladle soup into serving bowls. Serve with a sprinkle of grated Gruyere cheese.

Per Serving:
calories: 123 | fat: 9g | protein: 5g | carbs: 8g | net carbs: 6g | fiber: 2g

Hearty Cabbage and Pork Soup

Prep time: 10 minutes | Cook time: 12 minutes | Serves 3

- 1 teaspoon butter
- ½ cup shredded white cabbage
- ½ teaspoon ground coriander
- ½ teaspoon salt
- ½ teaspoon chili flakes
- 2 cups chicken broth
- ½ cup ground pork

1. Melt the butter in the Instant Pot on Sauté mode. 2. Add cabbage and sprinkle with ground coriander, salt, and chili flakes. 3. Fold in the chicken broth and ground pork. 4. Close the lid and select Manual mode. Set cooking time for 12 minutes on High Pressure. 5. When timer beeps, use a quick pressure release. Open the lid. 6. Ladle the soup and serve warm.

Per Serving:
calories: 350 | fat: 24g | protein: 30g | carbs: 1g | net carbs: 1g | fiber: 0g

Spicy Chili Lamb Soup

Prep time: 5 minutes | Cook time: 25 minutes | Serves 6

- 1 tablespoon coconut oil
- ¾ pound ground lamb
- 2 cups shredded cabbage
- ½ onion, chopped
- 2 teaspoons minced garlic
- 4 cups chicken broth
- 2 cups coconut milk
- 1½ tablespoons red chili paste or as much as you want
- Zest and juice of 1 lime
- 1 cup shredded kale

1. Cook the lamb. In a medium stockpot over medium-high heat, warm the coconut oil. Add the lamb and cook it, stirring it often, until it has browned, about 6 minutes. 2. Cook the vegetables. Add the cabbage, onion, and garlic and sauté until they've softened, about 5 minutes. 3. Simmer the soup. Stir in the chicken broth, coconut milk, red chili paste, lime zest, and lime juice. Bring it to a boil, then reduce the heat to low and simmer until the cabbage is tender, about 10 minutes. 4. Add the kale. Stir in the kale and simmer the soup for 3 more minutes. 5. Serve. Spoon the soup into six bowls and serve.

Per Serving:

calories: 380 | fat: 32g | protein: 17g | carbs: 7g | net carbs: 6g | fiber: 1g

Flavorful Chicken Enchilada Soup

Prep time: 10 minutes | Cook time: 40 minutes | Serves 6

- 2 (6-ounce / 170-g) boneless, skinless chicken breasts
- ½ tablespoon chili powder
- ½ teaspoon salt
- ½ teaspoon garlic powder
- ¼ teaspoon pepper
- ½ cup red enchilada sauce
- ½ medium onion, diced
- 1 (4-ounce / 113-g) can green chilies
- 2 cups chicken broth
- ⅛ cup pickled jalapeños
- 4 ounces (113 g) cream cheese
- 1 cup uncooked cauliflower rice
- 1 avocado, diced
- 1 cup shredded mild Cheddar cheese
- ½ cup sour cream

1. Sprinkle seasoning over chicken breasts and set aside. Pour enchilada sauce into Instant Pot and place chicken on top. 2. Add onion, chilies, broth, and jalapeños to the pot, then place cream cheese on top of chicken breasts. Click lid closed. Adjust time for 25 minutes. When timer beeps, quick-release the pressure and shred chicken with forks. 3. Mix soup together and add cauliflower rice,

with pot on Keep Warm setting. Replace lid and let pot sit for 15 minutes, still on Keep Warm. This will cook cauliflower rice. Serve with avocado, Cheddar, and sour cream.

Per Serving:

calories: 318 | fat: 19g | protein: 21g | carbs: 10g | net carbs: 7g | fiber: 3g

Creamy Broccoli Cheddar Soup

Prep time: 5 minutes | Cook time: 10 minutes | Serves 4

- 2 tablespoons butter
- ⅛ cup onion, diced
- ½ teaspoon garlic powder
- ½ teaspoon salt
- ¼ teaspoon pepper
- 2 cups chicken broth
- 1 cup chopped broccoli
- 1 tablespoon cream cheese, softened
- ¼ cup heavy cream
- 1 cup shredded Cheddar cheese

1. Press the Sauté button and add butter to Instant Pot. Add onion and sauté until translucent. Press the Cancel button and add garlic powder, salt, pepper, broth, and broccoli to pot. 2. Click lid closed. Press the Soup button and set time for 5 minutes. When timer beeps, stir in heavy cream, cream cheese, and Cheddar.

Per Serving:

calories: 250 | fat: 20g | protein: 9g | carbs: 4g | net carbs: 3g | fiber: 1g

Hearty Beef and Cauliflower Soup

Prep time: 10 minutes | Cook time: 14 minutes | Serves 4

- 1 cup ground beef
- ½ cup cauliflower, shredded
- 1 teaspoon unsweetened tomato purée
- ¼ cup coconut milk
- 1 teaspoon minced garlic
- 1 teaspoon dried oregano
- ½ teaspoon salt
- 4 cups water

1. Put all ingredients in the Instant Pot and stir well. 2. Close the lid. Select Manual mode and set cooking time for 14 minutes on High Pressure. 3. When timer beeps, make a quick pressure release and open the lid. 4. Blend with an immersion blender until smooth. 5. Serve warm.

Per Serving:

calories: 106 | fat: 8g | protein: 7g | carbs: 2g | net carbs: 1g | fiber: 1g

Cauliflower Soup with Crispy Bacon

- 2 tablespoon ghee
- 1 onion, chopped
- 2 head cauliflower, cut into florets
- 2 cups water
- Salt and black pepper to taste
- 3 cups almond milk
- 1 cup shredded white cheddar cheese
- 3 bacon strips

1. Melt the ghee in a saucepan over medium heat and sauté the onion for 3 minutes until fragrant. 2. Include the cauli florets, sauté for 3 minutes to slightly soften, add the water, and season with salt and black pepper. Bring to a boil, and then reduce the heat to low. Cover and cook for 10 minutes. Puree cauliflower with an immersion blender until the ingredients are evenly combined and stir in the almond milk and cheese until the cheese melts. Adjust taste with salt and black pepper. 3. In a non-stick skillet over high heat, fry the bacon, until crispy. Divide soup between serving bowls, top with crispy bacon, and serve hot.

Per Serving:

calories: 413 | fat: 32g | protein: 17g | carbs: 20g | net carbs: 15g | fiber: 7g

Creamy Cauliflower and Blue Cheese Soup

- 2 tablespoons extra-virgin avocado oil
- 1 small red onion, diced
- 1 medium celery stalk, sliced
- 1 medium cauliflower, cut into small florets
- 2 cups vegetable or chicken stock
- ¼ cup goat's cream or heavy
- whipping cream
- Salt and black pepper, to taste
- 1 cup crumbled goat's or sheep's blue cheese, such as Roquefort
- 2 tablespoons chopped fresh chives
- 5 tablespoons extra-virgin olive oil

1. Heat a medium saucepan greased with the avocado oil over medium heat. Sweat the onion and celery for 3 to 5 minutes, until soft and fragrant. Add the cauliflower florets and cook for

5 minutes. Add the vegetable stock and bring to a boil. Cook for about 10 minutes, or until the cauliflower is tender. Remove from the heat and let cool for a few minutes. 2. Add the cream. Use an immersion blender, or pour into a blender, to process until smooth and creamy. Season with salt and pepper to taste. Divide the soup between serving bowls and top with the crumbled blue cheese, chives, and olive oil. To store, let cool and refrigerate in a sealed container for up to 5 days.

Per Serving:

calories: 367 | fat: 31g | protein: 12g | carbs: 11g | net carbs: 8g | fiber: 3g

Hearty Venison and Tomato Stew

- 1 tablespoon unsalted butter
- 1 cup diced onions
- 2 cups button mushrooms, sliced in half
- 2 large stalks celery, cut into ¼-inch pieces
- Cloves squeezed from 2 heads roasted garlic or 4 cloves garlic, minced
- 2 pounds (907 g) boneless venison or beef roast, cut into 4 large pieces
- 5 cups beef broth
- 1 (14½-ounce / 411-g) can
- diced tomatoes
- 1 teaspoon fine sea salt
- 1 teaspoon ground black pepper
- ½ teaspoon dried rosemary, or 1 teaspoon fresh rosemary, finely chopped
- ½ teaspoon dried thyme leaves, or 1 teaspoon fresh thyme leaves, finely chopped
- ½ head cauliflower, cut into large florets
- Fresh thyme leaves, for garnish

1. Place the butter in the Instant Pot and press Sauté. Once melted, add the onions and sauté for 4 minutes, or until soft. 2. Add the mushrooms, celery, and garlic and sauté for another 3 minutes, or until the mushrooms are golden brown. Press Cancel to stop the Sauté. Add the roast, broth, tomatoes, salt, pepper, rosemary, and thyme. 3. Seal the lid, press Manual, and set the timer for 30 minutes. Once finished, turn the valve to venting for a quick release. 4. Add the cauliflower. Seal the lid, press Manual, and set the timer for 5 minutes. Once finished, let the pressure release naturally. 5. Remove the lid and shred the meat with two forks. Taste the liquid and add more salt, if needed. Ladle the stew into bowls. Garnish with thyme leaves.

Per Serving:

calories: 359 | fat: 21g | protein: 32g | carbs: 9g | net carbs: 6g | fiber: 3g

Timeless Chicken Soup

Prep time: 15 minutes | Cook time: 45 minutes | Serves 4

- 3 tablespoons olive oil
- 1 (14 ounces / 397 g) bag frozen peppers and onions
- 1 pound (454 g) chicken thigh meat, diced
- 1 tablespoon dried thyme
- ½ tablespoon garlic powder
- 1 teaspoon salt
- 1 teaspoon freshly ground black pepper
- 1 (32 ounces / 907 g) container chicken or vegetable broth, or bone broth
- ½ pound (227 g) spinach
- 1 teaspoon dried basil (optional)

1. Heat the oil in a large pot over medium heat. 2. Add the peppers and onions and cook until no longer frozen, 8 to 10 minutes. 3. Add the chicken and cook, stirring occasionally. 4. Stir in the thyme, garlic powder, salt, and pepper. Add the broth and cook for about 25 minutes. 5. Add the spinach and cook for another 5 minutes. 6. Serve the soup in bowls, sprinkled with the basil (if using).

Per Serving:
calories: 323 | fat: 19g | protein: 28g | carbs: 10g | net carbs: 7g | fiber: 3g

Rich and Creamy Mushroom Soup

Prep time: 10 minutes | Cook time: 30 minutes | Serves 4

- 2 slices bacon, cut into ¼-inch dice
- 2 tablespoons minced shallots or onions
- 1 teaspoon minced garlic
- 1 pound (454 g) button mushrooms, cleaned and quartered or sliced
- 1 teaspoon dried thyme
For Garnish:
- Fresh thyme leaves

- leaves
- 2 cups chicken bone broth, homemade or store-bought
- 1 teaspoon fine sea salt
- ½ teaspoon freshly ground black pepper
- 2 large eggs
- 2 tablespoons lemon juice

- MCT oil or extra-virgin olive oil, for drizzling

1. Place the diced bacon in a stockpot and sauté over medium heat until crispy, about 3 minutes. Remove the bacon from the pan, but leave the drippings. Add the shallots and garlic to the pan with the drippings and sauté over medium heat for about 3 minutes, until softened and aromatic. 2. Add the mushrooms and dried thyme and sauté over medium heat until the mushrooms are golden brown, about 10 minutes. Add the broth, salt, and pepper and bring to boil. 3. Whisk the eggs and lemon juice in a medium bowl. While whisking, very slowly pour in ½ cup of the hot soup (if you add the hot soup too quickly, the eggs will curdle). Slowly whisk another cup of the hot soup into the egg mixture. 4. Pour the hot egg mixture into the pot while stirring. Add the cooked bacon, then reduce the heat and simmer for 10 minutes, stirring constantly. The soup will thicken slightly as it cooks. Remove from the heat. Garnish with fresh thyme and drizzle with MCT oil before serving. 5. This soup is best served fresh but can be stored in an airtight container in the fridge for up to 3 days. To reheat, place in a saucepan over medium-low heat until warmed, stirring constantly to keep the eggs from curdling.

Per Serving:
calories: 185 | fat: 13g | protein: 11g | carbs: 6g | net carbs: 4g | fiber: 2g

Fresh Summer Vegetable Soup

Prep time: 10 minutes | Cook time: 6 minutes | Serves 6

- 3 cups finely sliced leeks
- 6 cups chopped rainbow chard, stems and leaves separated
- 1 cup chopped celery
- 2 tablespoons minced garlic, divided
- 1 teaspoon dried oregano
- 1 teaspoon salt
- 2 teaspoons freshly ground

- black pepper
- 3 cups chicken broth, plus more as needed
- 2 cups sliced yellow summer squash, ½-inch slices
- ¼ cup chopped fresh parsley
- ¾ cup heavy (whipping) cream
- 4 to 6 tablespoons grated Parmesan cheese

1. Put the leeks, chard, celery, 1 tablespoon of garlic, oregano, salt, pepper, and broth into the inner cooking pot of the Instant Pot. 2. Lock the lid into place. Select Manual and adjust the pressure to High. Cook for 3 minutes. When the cooking is complete, quick-release the pressure. Unlock the lid. 3. Add more broth if needed. 4. Turn the pot to Sauté and adjust the heat to high. Add the yellow squash, parsley, and remaining 1 tablespoon of garlic. 5. Allow the soup to cook for 2 to 3 minutes, or until the squash is softened and cooked through. 6. Stir in the cream and ladle the soup into bowls. Sprinkle with the Parmesan cheese and serve.

Per Serving:
calories: 210 | fat: 14g | protein: 10g | carbs: 12g | net carbs: 8g | fiber: 4g

Chicken Soup with Cauliflower Rice

Prep time: 5 minutes | Cook time: 20 minutes | Serves 4

- 4 tablespoons butter
- ¼ cup diced onion
- 2 stalks celery, chopped
- ½ cup fresh spinach
- ½ teaspoon salt
- ¼ teaspoon pepper
- ¼ teaspoon dried thyme
- ¼ teaspoon dried parsley
- 1 bay leaf
- 2 cups chicken broth
- 2 cups diced cooked chicken
- ¾ cup uncooked cauliflower rice
- ½ teaspoon xanthan gum (optional)

1. Press the Sauté button and add butter to Instant Pot. Add onions and sauté until translucent. Place celery and spinach into Instant Pot and sauté for 2 to 3 minutes until spinach is wilted. Press the Cancel button. 2. Sprinkle seasoning into Instant Pot and add bay leaf, broth, and cooked chicken. Click lid closed. Press the Soup button and adjust time for 10 minutes. 3. When timer beeps, quick-release the pressure and stir in cauliflower rice. Leave Instant Pot on Keep Warm setting to finish cooking cauliflower rice additional 10 minutes. Serve warm. 4. For a thicker soup, stir in xanthan gum.

Per Serving:

calories: 228 | fat: 14g | protein: 22g | carbs: 3g | net carbs: 2g | fiber: 1g

Hearty Beef and Mushroom Stew

Prep time: 15 minutes | Cook time: 30 minutes | Serves 4

- 2 tablespoons coconut oil
- 1 pound (454 g) cubed chuck roast
- 1 cup sliced button mushrooms
- ½ medium onion, chopped
- 2 cups beef broth
- ½ cup chopped celery
- 1 tablespoon sugar-free tomato paste
- 1 teaspoon thyme
- 2 garlic cloves, minced
- ½ teaspoon xanthan gum

1. Press the Sauté button and add coconut oil to Instant Pot. Brown cubes of chuck roast until golden, working in batches if necessary. (If the pan is overcrowded, they will not brown properly.) Set aside after browning is completed. 2. Add mushrooms and onions to pot. Sauté until mushrooms begin to brown and onions are translucent. Press the Cancel button. 3. Add broth to Instant Pot. Use wooden spoon to scrape bits from bottom if necessary. Add celery, tomato paste, thyme, and garlic. Click lid closed. Press the Manual button and adjust time for 35 minutes. When timer beeps, allow a natural release. 4. When pressure valve drops, stir in xanthan gum and allow to thicken. Serve warm.

Per Serving:

calories: 354 | fat: 25g | protein: 24g | carbs: 4g | net carbs: 2g | fiber: 2g

Flavorful Beef and Eggplant Tagine

Prep time: 15 minutes | Cook time: 25 minutes | Serves 6

- 1 pound (454 g) beef fillet, chopped
- 1 eggplant, chopped
- 6 ounces (170 g) scallions, chopped
- 4 cups beef broth
- 1 teaspoon ground allspices
- 1 teaspoon erythritol
- 1 teaspoon coconut oil

1. Put all ingredients in the Instant Pot. Stir to mix well. 2. Close the lid. Select Manual mode and set cooking time for 25 minutes on High Pressure. 3. When timer beeps, use a natural pressure release for 15 minutes, then release any remaining pressure. Open the lid. 4. Serve warm.

Per Serving:

calories: 158 | fat: 5g | protein: 21g | carbs: 8g | net carbs: 5g | fiber: 4g

Creamy Parmesan Zucchini Soup

Prep time: 10 minutes | Cook time: 1 minute | Serves 2

- 1 zucchini, grated
- 1 teaspoon ground paprika
- ½ teaspoon cayenne pepper
- ½ cup coconut milk
- 1 cup beef broth
- 1 tablespoon dried cilantro
- 1 ounce (28 g) Parmesan, grated

1. Put the grated zucchini, paprika, cayenne pepper, coconut milk, beef broth, and dried cilantro in the instant pot. 2. Close and seal the lid. 3. Cook the soup on Manual (High Pressure) for 1 minute. Make a quick pressure release. 4. Ladle the soup in the serving bowls and top with Parmesan.

Per Serving:

calories: 223 | fat: 18g | protein: 10g | carbs: 8g | net carbs: 5g | fiber: 3g

Classic New England Clam Chowder

- ¼ pound uncured bacon, chopped
- 2 tablespoons grass-fed butter
- ½ onion, finely chopped
- 1 celery stalk, chopped
- 2 teaspoons minced garlic
- 2 tablespoons arrowroot
- 4 cups fish or chicken stock
- 1 teaspoon chopped fresh thyme
- 2 bay leaves
- 3 (6½-ounce) cans clams, drained
- 1½ cups heavy (whipping) cream
- Sea salt, for seasoning
- Freshly ground black pepper, for seasoning
- 2 tablespoons chopped fresh parsley

1. Cook the bacon. In a medium stockpot over medium-high heat, fry the bacon until it's crispy. Transfer the bacon with a slotted spoon to a plate and set it aside. 2. Sauté the vegetables. Melt the butter in the stockpot, add the onion, celery, and garlic and sauté them until they've softened, about 3 minutes. Whisk in the arrowroot and cook for 1 minute. Add the stock, thyme, and bay leaves and bring the soup to just before it boils. Then reduce the heat to medium-low and simmer until the soup thickens, about 10 minutes. 3. Finish the soup. Stir in the clams and cream and simmer the soup until it's heated through, about 5 minutes. Find and throw out the bay leaves. 4. Serve. Season the chowder with salt and pepper. Ladle it into bowls, garnish with the parsley, and crumbles of the bacon, then serve.

Per Serving:

calories: 384 | fat: 28g | protein: 23g | carbs: 6g | net carbs: 6g | fiber: 2g

Fresh Green Garden Soup

- 1 tablespoon olive oil
- 1 garlic clove, diced
- ½ cup cauliflower florets
- 1 cup kale, chopped
- 2 tablespoons chives, chopped
- 1 teaspoon sea salt
- 6 cups beef broth

1. Heat the olive oil in the Instant Pot on Sauté mode for 2 minutes and add the garlic. Sauté for 2 minutes or until fragrant. 2. Add cauliflower, kale, chives, sea salt, and beef broth. 3. Close the lid. Select Manual mode and set cooking time for 5 minutes on High Pressure. 4. When timer beeps, use a quick pressure release and open the lid. 5. Ladle the soup into the bowls. Serve warm.

Per Serving:

calories: 80 | fat: 5g | protein: 7g | carbs: 2g | net carbs: 2g | fiber: 1g

Hearty Tomato and Basil Parmesan Soup

- 2 tablespoons unsalted butter or coconut oil
- ½ cup finely diced onions
- Cloves squeezed from 1 head roasted garlic , or 2 cloves garlic, minced
- 1 tablespoon dried basil leaves
- 1 teaspoon dried oregano leaves
- 1 (8 ounces / 227 g) package cream cheese, softened
- 4 cups chicken broth
- 2 (14½ ounces / 411 g) cans diced tomatoes
- 1 cup shredded Parmesan cheese, plus more for garnish
- 1 teaspoon fine sea salt
- ¼ teaspoon ground black pepper
- Fresh basil leaves, for garnish

1. Place the butter in the Instant Pot and press Sauté. Once melted, add the onions, garlic, basil, and oregano and cook, stirring often, for 4 minutes, or until the onions are soft. Press Cancel to stop the Sauté. 2. Add the cream cheese and whisk to loosen. (If you don't use a whisk to loosen the cream cheese, you will end up with clumps in your soup.) Slowly whisk in the broth. Add the tomatoes, Parmesan, salt, and pepper and stir to combine. 3. Seal the lid, press Manual, and set the timer for 8 minutes. Once finished, turn the valve to venting for a quick release. 4. Remove the lid and purée the soup with a stick blender, or transfer the soup to a regular blender or food processor and process until smooth. If using a regular blender, you may need to blend the soup in two batches; if you overfill the blender jar, the soup will not purée properly. 5. Season with salt and pepper to taste, if desired. Ladle the soup into bowls and garnish with more Parmesan and basil leaves.

Per Serving:

calories: 146 | fat: 10g | protein: 8g | carbs: 4g | net carbs: 3g | fiber: 1g

Spicy Avocado and Serrano Chile Soup

- 2 avocados
- 1 small fresh tomatillo, quartered
- 2 cups chicken broth
- 2 tablespoons avocado oil
- 1 tablespoon butter
- 2 tablespoons finely minced onion
- 1 clove garlic, minced
- ½ Serrano chile, deseeded and ribs removed, minced, plus thin slices for garnish
- ¼ teaspoon sea salt
- Pinch of ground white pepper
- ½ cup full-fat coconut milk
- Fresh cilantro sprigs, for garnish

1. Scoop the avocado flesh into a food processor. Add the tomatillo and chicken broth and purée until smooth. Set aside. 2. Set the Instant Pot to Sauté mode and add the avocado oil and butter. When the butter melts, add the onion and garlic and sauté for a minute or until softened. Add the Serrano chile and sauté for 1 minute more. 3. Pour the puréed avocado mixture into the pot, add the salt and pepper, and stir to combine. 4. Secure the lid. Press the Manual button and set cooking time for 5 minutes on High Pressure. 5. When timer beeps, use a quick pressure release. Open the lid and stir in the coconut milk. 6. Serve hot topped with thin slices of Serrano chile, and cilantro sprigs.

Per Serving:

calories: 333 | fat: 32g | protein: 4g | carbs: 15g | net carbs: 7g | fiber: 8g

Flavorful Cabbage Soup

- 1 tablespoon olive oil
- 3 garlic cloves, minced
- 1 onion, diced
- 3 carrots, diced
- 1 celery stalk, diced
- ½ green bell pepper, diced
- Salt and freshly ground black pepper, to taste
- 1 cup chopped kale
- 2 tablespoons tomato paste
- 2 (32-ounce / 907-g) cartons chicken broth
- 1 large head cabbage, chopped
- 1 teaspoon dried oregano
- 1 teaspoon dried thyme
- Grated Parmesan cheese, for topping

1. In a large saucepan over medium heat, heat the olive oil. 2. Add the garlic and onion. Sauté for 5 minutes. 3. Add the carrots and celery. Cook for 5 to 7 minutes until softened. 4. Add the bell pepper and stir well to combine. Cook for 5 to 7 minutes more. Season with salt and pepper and add the kale. 5. Stir in the tomato paste until well combined. 6. Pour in the chicken broth and bring the soup to a gentle boil. 7. Add the cabbage, oregano, and thyme. Season with more salt and pepper. Reduce the heat to low, cover the pan, and simmer for 15 minutes (a little longer if you have the time). Ladle into bowls and top with Parmesan before serving.

Per Serving:

calories: 156 | fat: 5g | protein: 10g | carbs: 23g | net carbs: 16g | fiber: 7g

Creamy Shrimp Chowder

- ¼ cup (60 ml) refined avocado oil or melted ghee (if tolerated)
- 1⅔ cups (140 g) diced mushrooms
- ⅓ cup (55 g) diced yellow onions
- 10½ ounces (300 g) small raw shrimp, shelled and deveined
- 1 can (13½ ounces/400 ml) full-fat coconut milk
- ⅓ cup (80 ml) chicken bone broth
- 2 tablespoons apple cider
- vinegar
- 1 teaspoon onion powder
- 1 teaspoon paprika
- 1 bay leaf
- ¾ teaspoon finely ground gray sea salt
- ½ teaspoon dried oregano leaves
- ¼ teaspoon ground black pepper
- 12 radishes (about 6 ounces/170 g), cubed
- 1 medium zucchini (about 7 ounces/200 g), cubed

1. Heat the avocado oil in a large saucepan on medium for a couple of minutes, then add the mushrooms and onions. Sauté for 8 to 10 minutes, until the onions are translucent and mushrooms are beginning to brown. 2. Add the remaining ingredients, except the radishes and zucchini. Cover and bring to a boil, then reduce the heat to low and simmer for 20 minutes. 3. After 20 minutes, add the radishes and zucchini. Continue to cook for 10 minutes, until the vegetables are fork-tender. 4. Remove the bay leaf, divide among 6 small soup bowls, and enjoy.

Per Serving:

calories: 301 | fat: 23g | protein: 14g | carbs: 7g | net carbs: 5g | fiber: 2g

Ramen Soup with Spaghetti Squash

Prep time: 15 minutes | Cook time: 1 hour | Serves 4

Spaghetti Squash:

- 1 medium (2-pound / 907-g) spaghetti squash
- 2 tablespoons avocado oil

- Sea salt, to taste

Soup:

- 1 tablespoon avocado oil
- 4 cloves garlic, minced
- 1 tablespoon minced fresh ginger
- 2 cups (5 ounces / 142 g) shiitake mushrooms, sliced

- 8 cups chicken broth
- ⅓ cup coconut aminos
- 1 tablespoon fish sauce (optional)
- 1½ teaspoons sea salt, or to taste

Garnishes:

- ¼ cup (0.9 ounce / 26 g) chopped green onions

- 4 large eggs, soft-boiled, peeled, and cut in half

1. Preheat the oven to 425ºF (220ºC). Line a baking sheet with foil and grease lightly. 2. Prepare the spaghetti squash: Use a sharp chef's knife to slice the spaghetti squash in half. To make it easier, use the knife to score where you'll be cutting first, then slice. Cut crosswise to yield longer noodles, or lengthwise for shorter ones. Scoop out the seeds. 3. Drizzle the inside of the halves with the avocado oil. Sprinkle lightly with sea salt. 4. Place the spaghetti squash halves on the lined baking sheet cut side down. Roast for 25 to 35 minutes, until the skin pierces easily with a knife. The knife should be able to go in pretty deep with very slight resistance. 5. Remove from the oven and let the squash rest on the pan (cut side down, without moving) for 10 minutes. Then use a fork to release the strands inside the shells and set aside. 6. Meanwhile, make the soup: In a large soup pot, heat the oil over medium heat. Add the garlic and ginger and sauté for about 1 minute, until fragrant. 7. Add the shiitake mushrooms and sauté for about 5 minutes, or until the mushrooms are soft. 8. Add the chicken broth, coconut aminos, and fish sauce (if using). Add salt to taste (start with 1 teaspoon salt and add more if needed, but I recommend 1½ teaspoons). Bring to a boil, then reduce the heat and simmer for 10 minutes. 9. Add the spaghetti squash noodles to the pot and simmer for 10 to 15 minutes, until hot and flavors develop to your liking. 10. Pour into bowls. Garnish with the green onions and soft-boiled eggs.

Per Serving:

calories: 238 | fat: 16g | protein: 10g | carbs: 10g | net carbs: 10g | fiber: 0g

Appendix 1:

Measurement Conversion Chart

VOLUME EQUIVALENTS(DRY)

US STANDARD	METRIC (APPROXIMATE)
1/8 teaspoon	0.5 mL
1/4 teaspoon	1 mL
1/2 teaspoon	2 mL
3/4 teaspoon	4 mL
1 teaspoon	5 mL
1 tablespoon	15 mL
1/4 cup	59 mL
1/2 cup	118 mL
3/4 cup	177 mL
1 cup	235 mL
2 cups	475 mL
3 cups	700 mL
4 cups	1 L

VOLUME EQUIVALENTS(LIQUID)

US STANDARD	US STANDARD (OUNCES)	METRIC (APPROXIMATE)
2 tablespoons	1 fl.oz.	30 mL
1/4 cup	2 fl.oz.	60 mL
1/2 cup	4 fl.oz.	120 mL
1 cup	8 fl.oz.	240 mL
1 1/2 cup	12 fl.oz.	355 mL
2 cups or 1 pint	16 fl.oz.	475 mL
4 cups or 1 quart	32 fl.oz.	1 L
1 gallon	128 fl.oz.	4 L

TEMPERATURES EQUIVALENTS

FAHRENHEIT(F)	CELSIUS(C) (APPROXIMATE)
225 °F	107 °C
250 °F	120 °C
275 °F	135 °C
300 °F	150 °C
325 °F	160 °C
350 °F	180 °C
375 °F	190 °C
400 °F	205 °C
425 °F	220 °C
450 °F	235 °C
475 °F	245 °C
500 °F	260 °C

WEIGHT EQUIVALENTS

US STANDARD	METRIC (APPROXIMATE)
1 ounce	28 g
2 ounces	57 g
5 ounces	142 g
10 ounces	284 g
15 ounces	425 g
16 ounces (1 pound)	455 g
1.5 pounds	680 g
2 pounds	907 g

Appendix 2:

The Dirty Dozen and Clean Fifteen

The Environmental Working Group (EWG) is a nonprofit, nonpartisan organization dedicated to protecting human health and the environment Its mission is to empower people to live healthier lives in a healthier environment. This organization publishes an annual list of the twelve kinds of produce, in sequence, that have the highest amount of pesticide residue-the Dirty Dozen-as well as a list of the fifteen kinds ofproduce that have the least amount of pesticide residue-the Clean Fifteen.

THE DIRTY DOZEN	THE CLEAN FIFTEEN
• The 2016 Dirty Dozen includes the following produce. These are considered among the year's most important produce to buy organic:	• The least critical to buy organically are the Clean Fifteen list. The following are on the 2016 list:

Strawberries	Spinach	Avocados	Papayas
Apples	Tomatoes	Corn	Kiw
Nectarines	Bell peppers	Pineapples	Eggplant
Peaches	Cherry tomatoes	Cabbage	Honeydew
Celery	Cucumbers	Sweet peas	Grapefruit
Grapes	Kale/collard greens	Onions	Cantaloupe
Cherries	Hot peppers	Asparagus	Cauliflower
		Mangos	

THE DIRTY DOZEN	THE CLEAN FIFTEEN
• The Dirty Dozen list contains two additional itemskale/collard greens and hot peppers-because they tend to contain trace levels of highly hazardous pesticides.	• Some of the sweet corn sold in the United States are made from genetically engineered (GE) seedstock. Buy organic varieties of these crops to avoid GE produce.

Appendix 3:

Recipes Index

Made in the USA
Columbia, SC
07 May 2025

57644845R00059